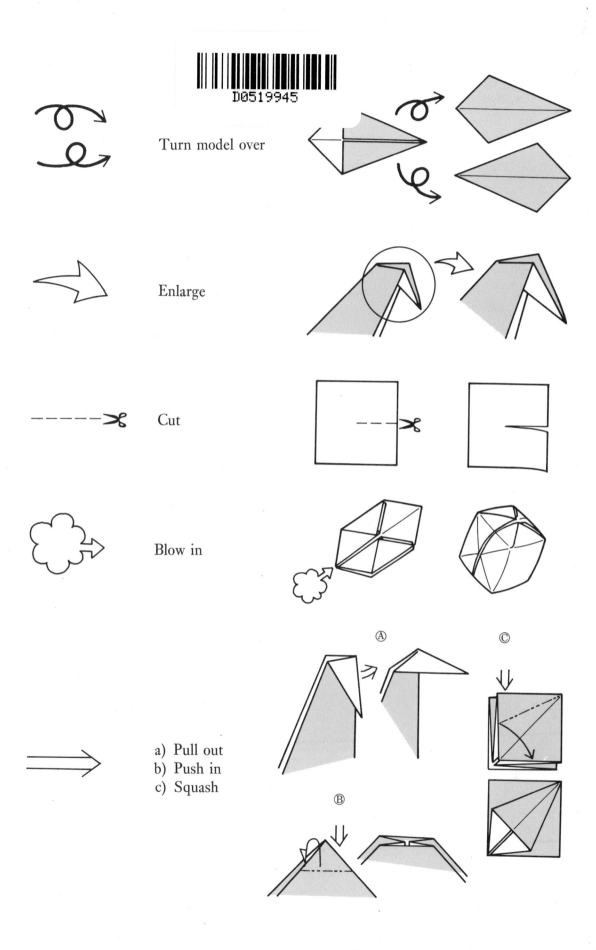

Turn model over

Enlarge

Cut

Blow in

a) Pull out
b) Push in
c) Squash

Ⓐ

Ⓑ

Ⓒ

THE JOY OF
ORIGAMI

Toshie Takahama

SHUFUNOTOMO / JAPAN PUBLICATIONS

Tokyo, Japan

10

© Copyright in Japan 1985 by Toshie Takahama

Published by Shufunotomo Co., Ltd.
2-9, Kanda Surugadai, Chiyoda-ku, Tokyo, 101 Japan

Distributors:
UNITED STATES: Kodansha America, Inc. through Farrar,
    Straus & Giroux, 19 Union Square West, New York, NY 10003.
CANADA: Fitzhenry & Whiteside Ltd., 91 Granton Drive,
    Richmond Hill, Ontario L4B 2N5.
BRITISH ISLES AND EUROPEAN CONTINENT: Premier Book
    Marketing Ltd., 1 Gower Street, London WC1E 6HA.
AUSTRALIA AND NEW ZEALAND: Bookwise International,
    54 Crittenden Road, Findon, South Australia 5023.
THE FAR EAST AND JAPAN: Japan Publications Trading Co., Ltd.,
    1-2-1, Sarugaku-cho, Chiyoda-ku, Tokyo 101.

ISBN 0-87040-603-5
Printed in Japan

INTRODUCTION

Paper-folding, "ORIGAMI" in Japanese, can be enjoyed by everybody. Nowadays in many parts of the world, people of all ages and from various backgrounds are folding paper for pleasure.

We can easily imagine that the first people to discover how to fold paper were the ancient inventors of paper. In Japan, the art of folding paper originated and developed in religious circles. Out of this ceremonial function grew a kind of paper-folding more familiar to the average person, paper-folding as play, which included making such things as animals, birds, and flowers. Various ways, both simple and complex, of folding paper for pleasure were passed down by mothers to their daughters for many, many generations in Japan.

This book will introduce you to some of these traditional models as well as new innovations. If ORIGAMI is something new for you, it is good to begin it with this book. If you are already accomplished at paper-folding, you will surely be excited when you find new folds, and discover the greater pleasure of creating more complex models by using the techniques you have already learned.

Look at each diagram carefully and read the instructions, looking ahead at the same time to the next diagram to see what shape will come as the result of the step you are working.

TOSHIE TAKAHAMA

CONTENTS

The Joy of Origami

Procedures

Inside Reverse Fold

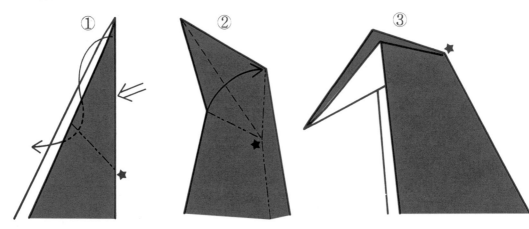

Outside Reverse Fold

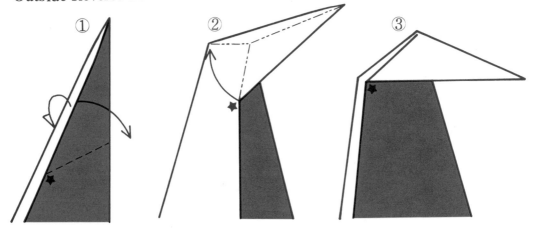

Crimps

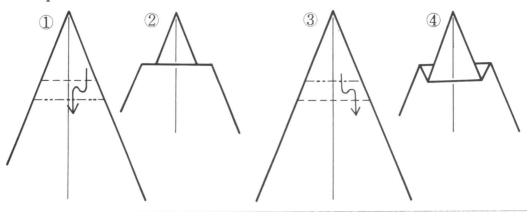

Making Feet

Making Beaks

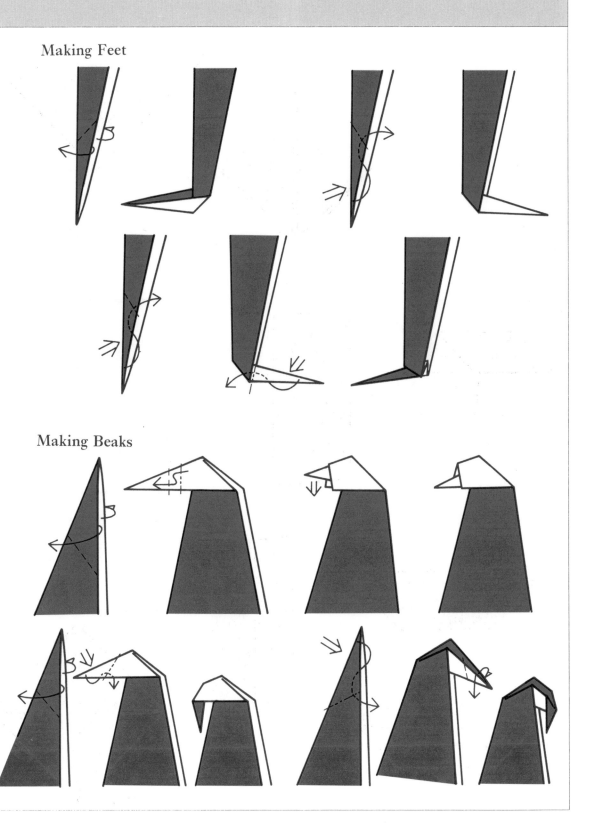

Basic Folds

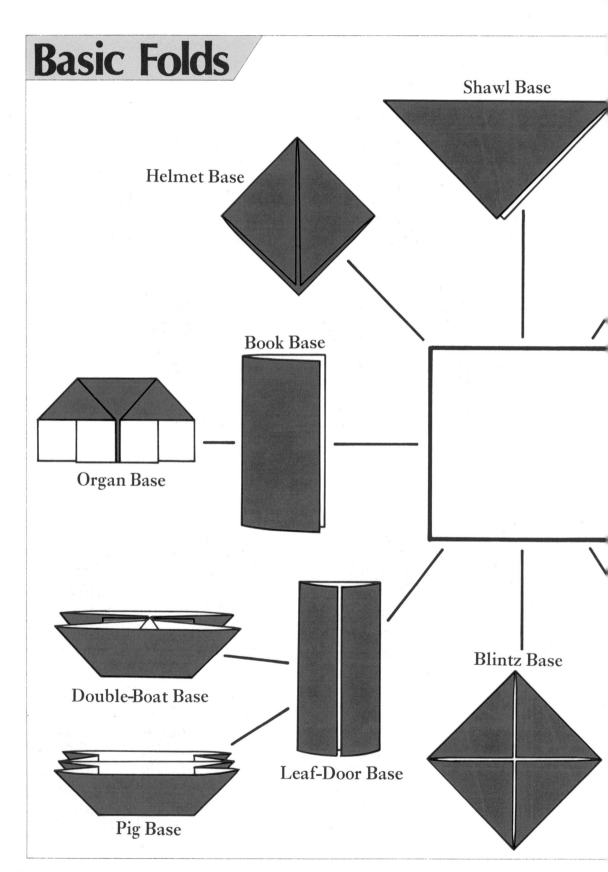

Shawl Base

Helmet Base

Book Base

Organ Base

Double-Boat Base

Leaf-Door Base

Pig Base

Blintz Base

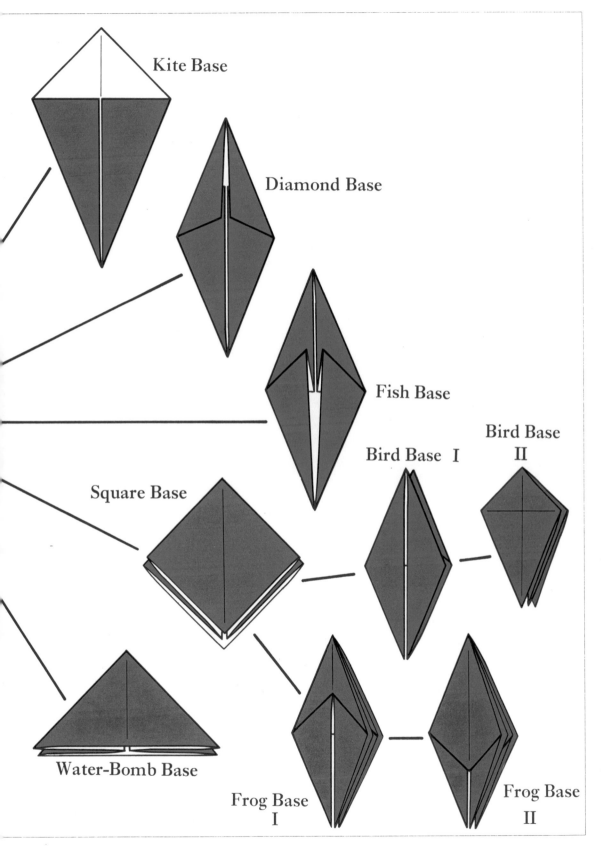

Kite Base

Diamond Base

Fish Base

Bird Base I

Bird Base II

Square Base

Water-Bomb Base

Frog Base I

Frog Base II

Folding Bases

Book Base

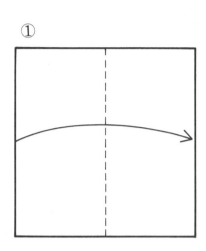

①

Fold this side to the right.

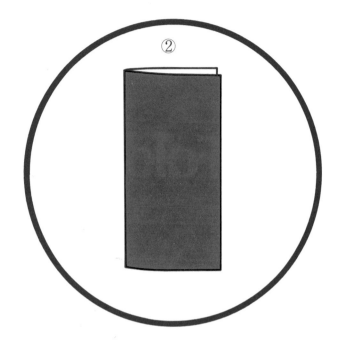

②

This is **Book Base.**

Leaf-Door Base

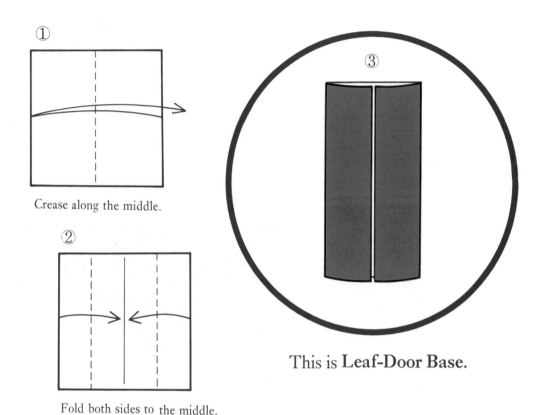

① Crease along the middle.

② Fold both sides to the middle.

③

This is **Leaf-Door Base.**

Shawl Base

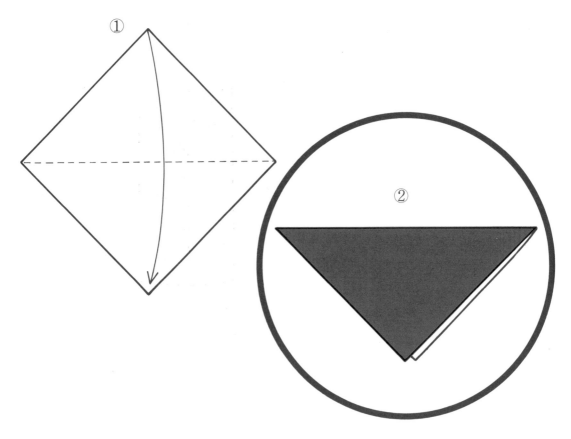

This is **Shawl Base.**

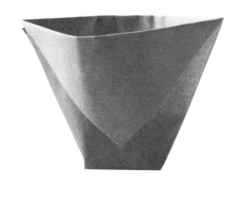

Helmet Base

① Begin with **Shawl Base** (p. 14).

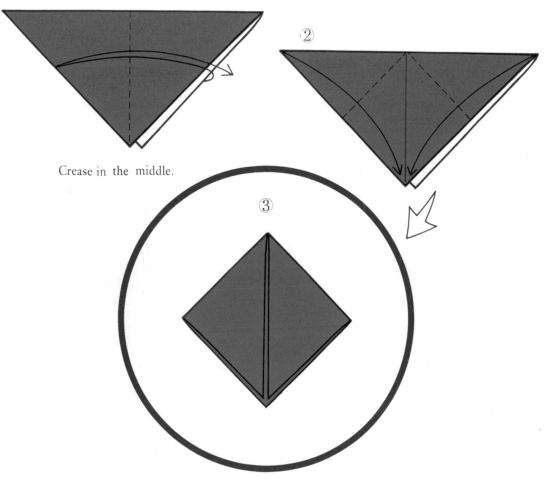

Crease in the middle.

② ③

This is **Helmet Base**.

Kite Base

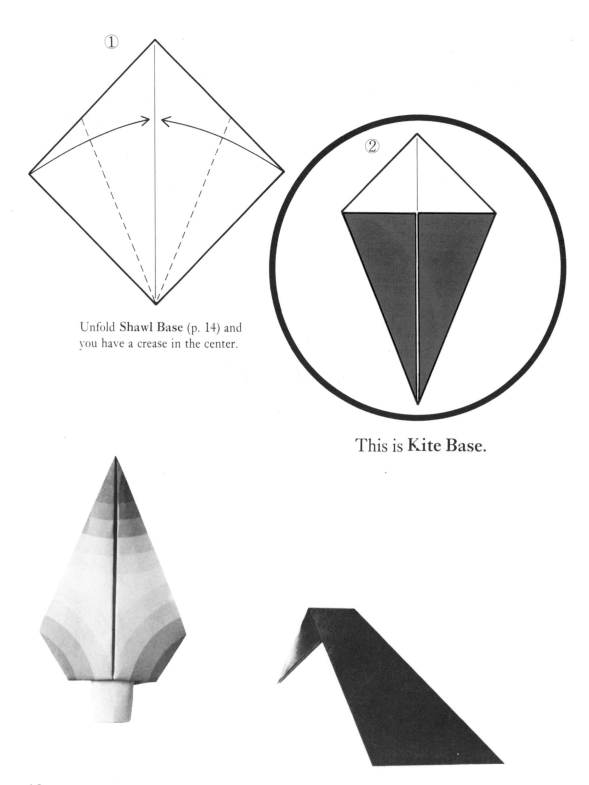

① Unfold **Shawl Base** (p. 14) and you have a crease in the center.

② This is **Kite Base**.

Diamond Base

Begin with **Kite Base** (p. 16).

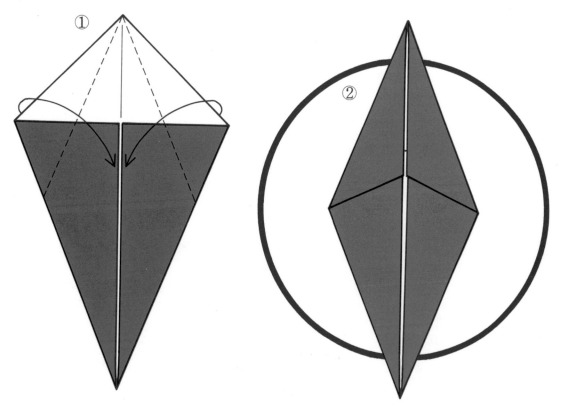

This is **Diamond Base**.

Blintz Base

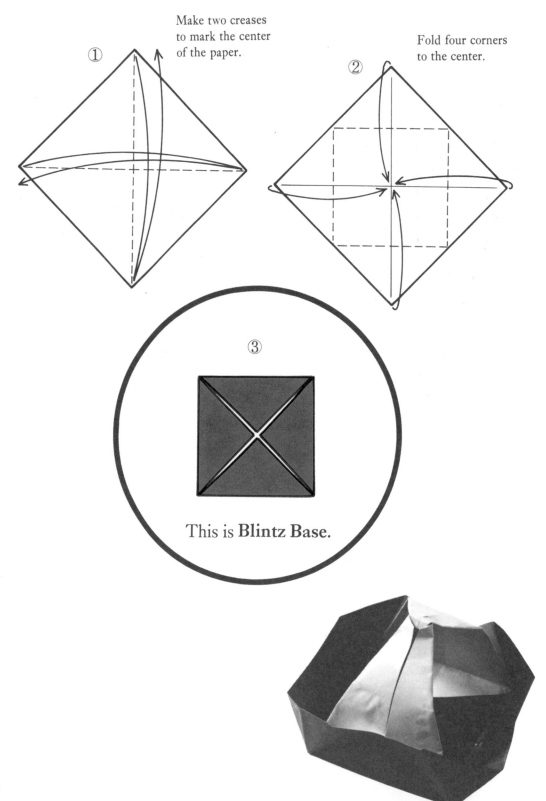

Make two creases to mark the center of the paper.

①

Fold four corners to the center.

②

③

This is **Blintz Base**.

Organ Base

Organ Base
Begin with **Book Base** (p. 12).

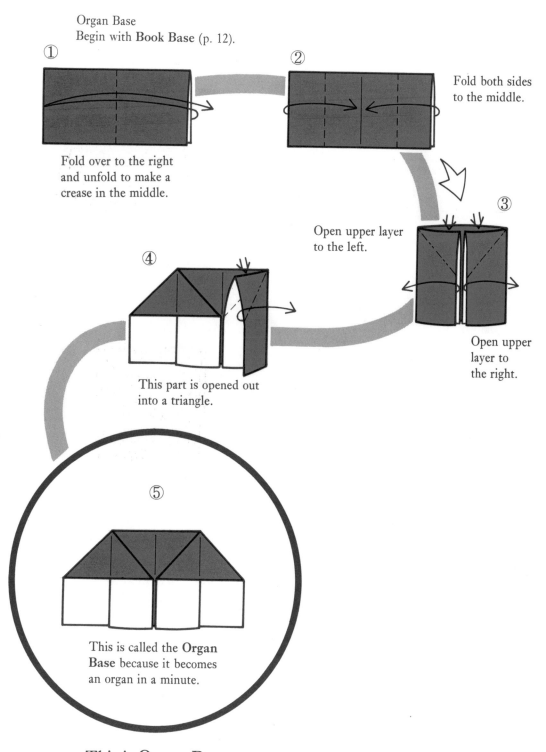

① Fold over to the right and unfold to make a crease in the middle.

② Fold both sides to the middle.

③ Open upper layer to the left.

Open upper layer to the right.

④ This part is opened out into a triangle.

⑤ This is called the **Organ Base** because it becomes an organ in a minute.

This is **Organ Base.**

Square Base

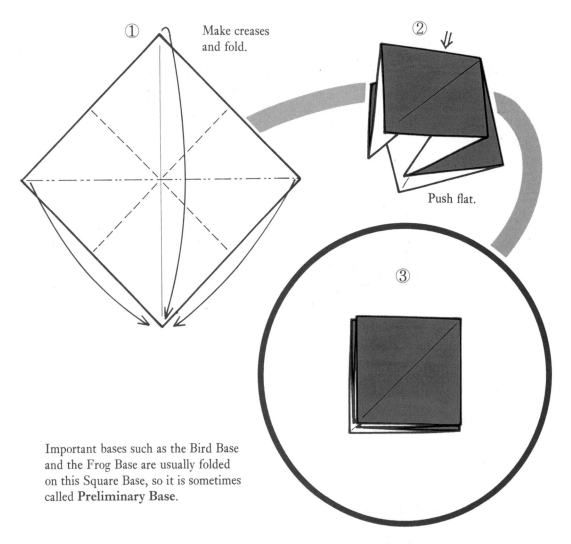

① Make creases and fold.

② Push flat.

③ This is **Square Base.**

Important bases such as the Bird Base and the Frog Base are usually folded on this Square Base, so it is sometimes called **Preliminary Base**.

Water-Bomb Base

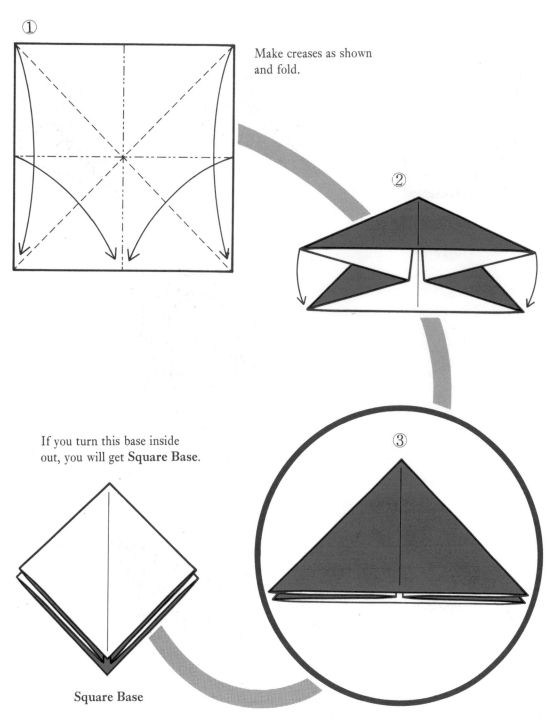

① Make creases as shown and fold.

②

③

If you turn this base inside out, you will get **Square Base**.

Square Base

This is **Water-Bomb Base**.

Bird Base

Begin with **Square Base** (p. 20).

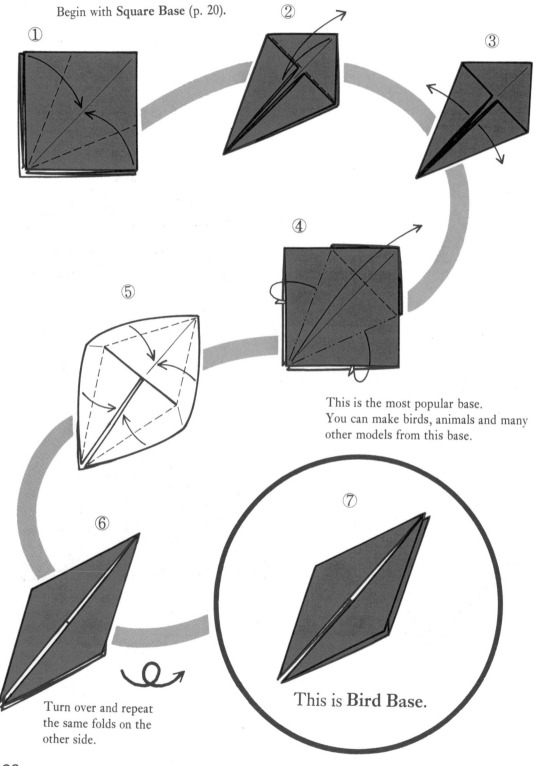

This is the most popular base.
You can make birds, animals and many
other models from this base.

This is **Bird Base**.

Turn over and repeat
the same folds on the
other side.

Fish Base

Begin with **Kite Base** (p. 16).

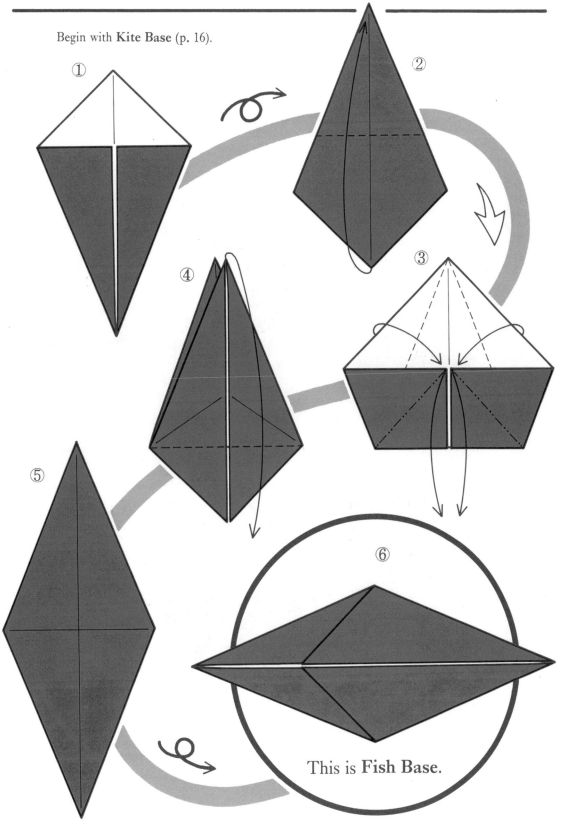

This is **Fish Base**.

Double-Boat Base

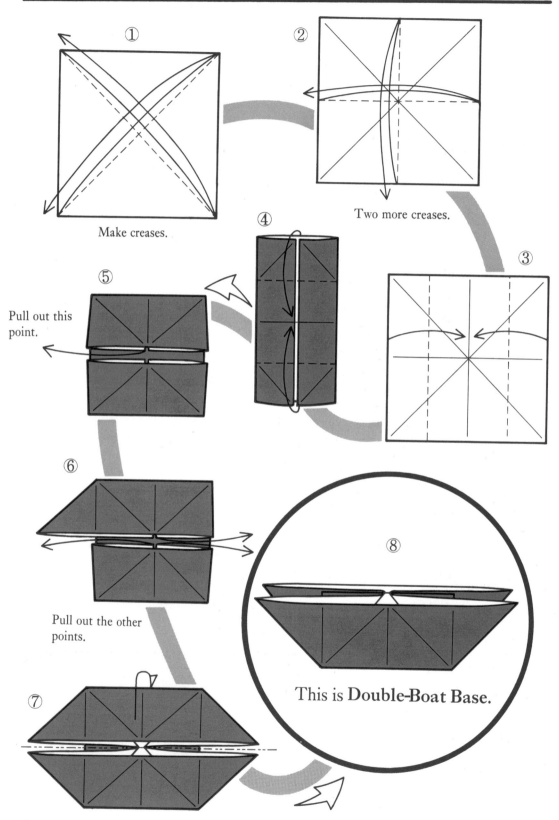

① Make creases.

② Two more creases.

③

④

⑤ Pull out this point.

⑥ Pull out the other points.

⑦

⑧ This is **Double-Boat Base.**

24

Pig Base

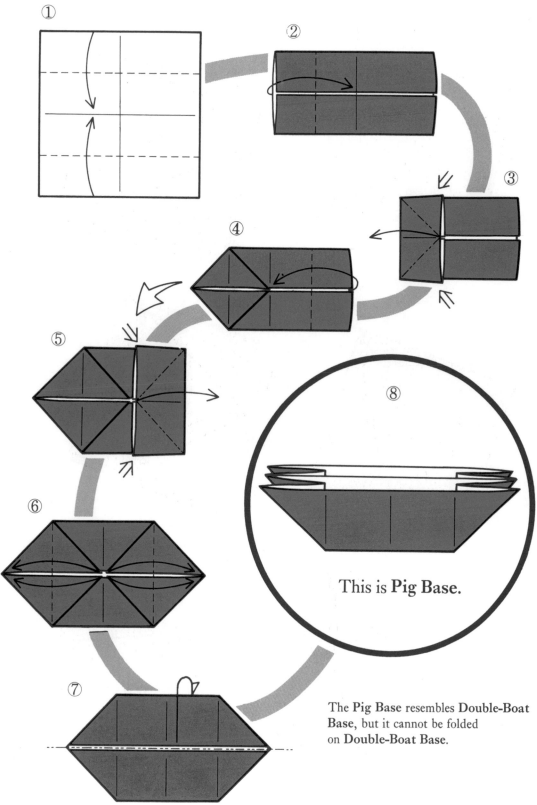

① ② ③ ④ ⑤ ⑥ ⑦ ⑧

This is **Pig Base.**

The **Pig Base** resembles **Double-Boat Base,** but it cannot be folded on **Double-Boat Base.**

Frog Base

Begin with **Square Base** (p. 20).

① Squash.

②

④

③

⑤

⑥

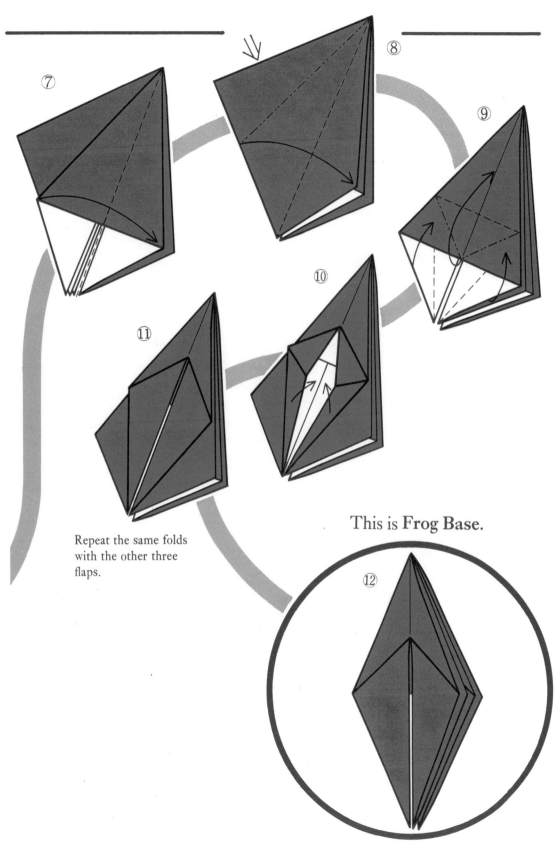

⑦

⑧

⑨

⑩

⑪

Repeat the same folds with the other three flaps.

This is **Frog Base.**

⑫

The Joy of Origami

Yachts	Begin with **Shawl Base** (p. 14).

Yacht I

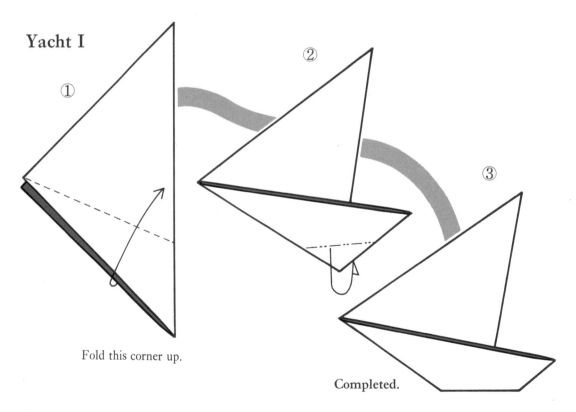

① Fold this corner up.

②

③ Completed.

Begin with Fig. ② of **Yacht I** (p. 30).

Yacht II

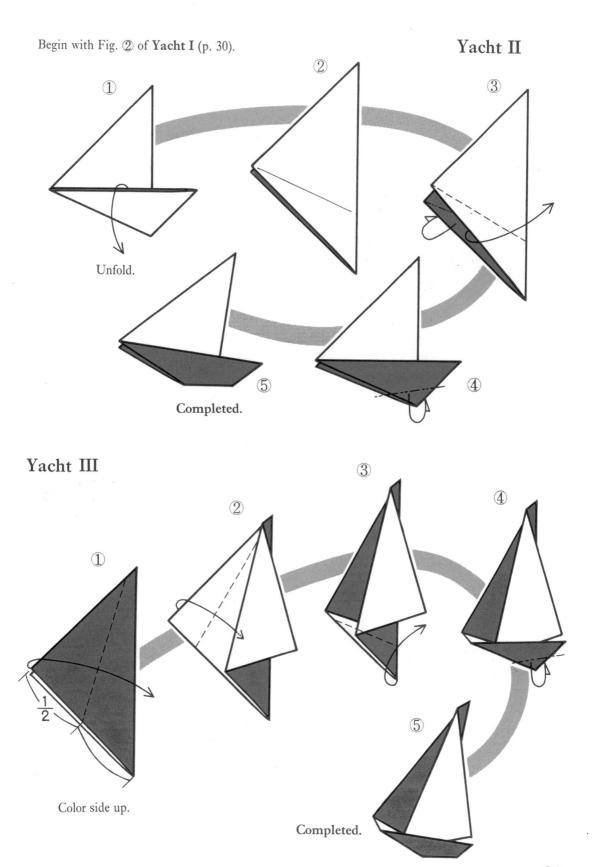

① Unfold.

②

③

④

⑤ Completed.

Yacht III

① Color side up. $\frac{1}{2}$

②

③

④

⑤ Completed.

Grasshopper | Begin with **Shawl Base** (p. 14).

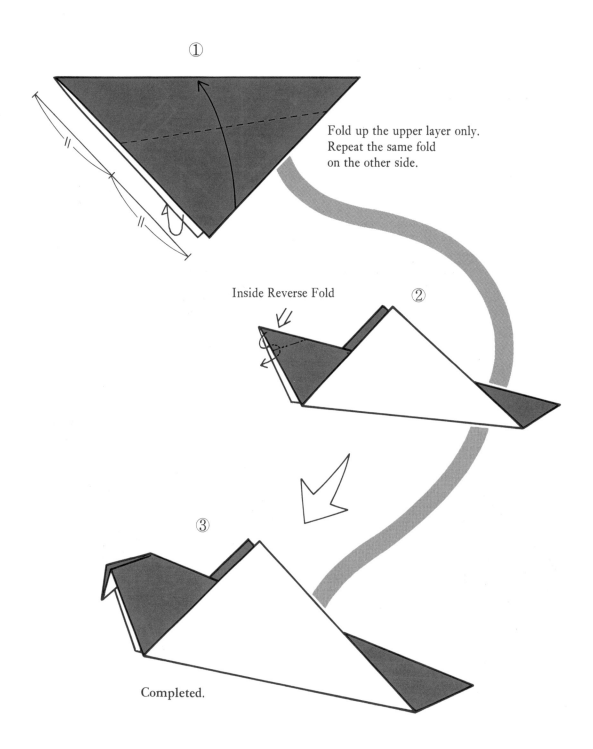

①

Fold up the upper layer only.
Repeat the same fold
on the other side.

Inside Reverse Fold

②

③

Completed.

Sea Gull

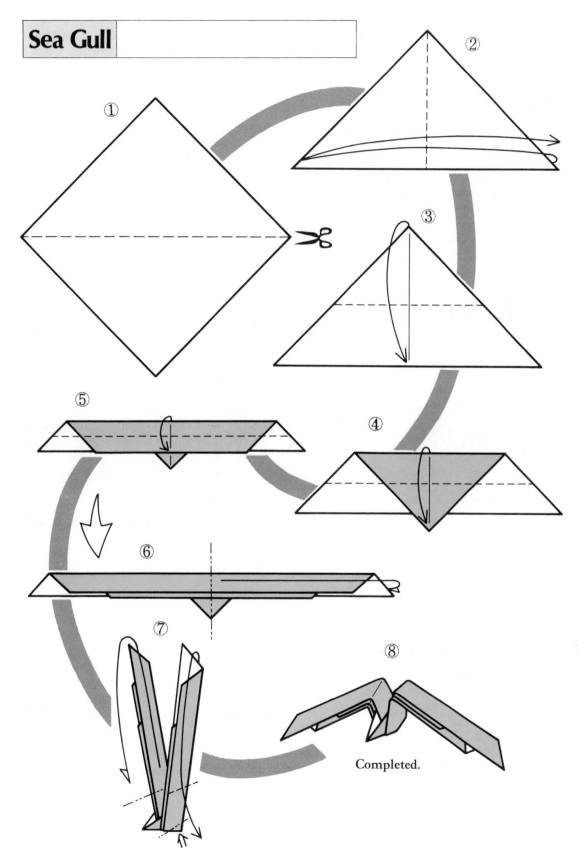

Completed.

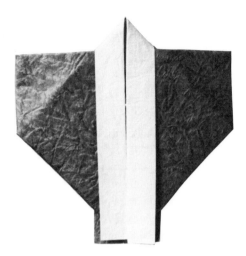

Undershirt | Begin with **Book Base** (p. 12). (Japanese traditional)

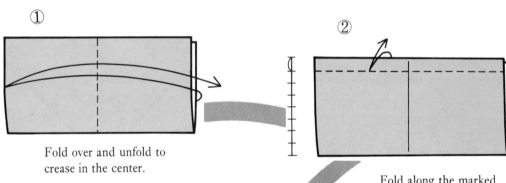

① Fold over and unfold to crease in the center.

② Fold along the marked line and unfold.

③

④ Fold upper flap only to this side.

Make the same fold on the other side.

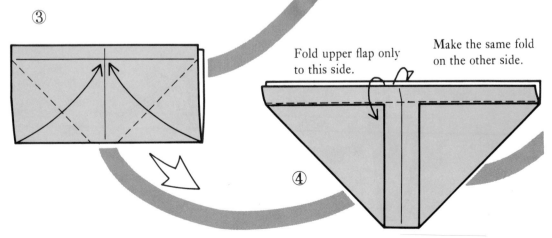

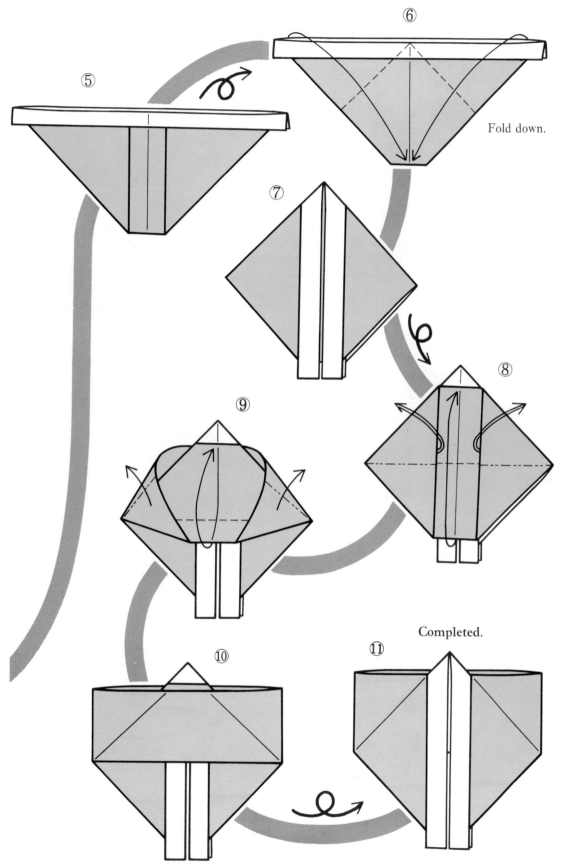

⑥

⑤

Fold down.

⑦

⑧

⑨

Completed.

⑩

⑪

35

Cup

Begin with **Shawl Base** (p. 14).

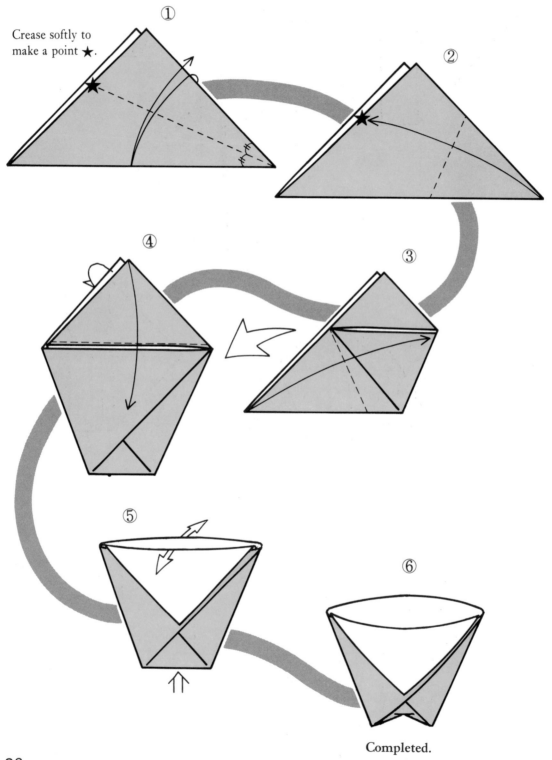

Crease softly to make a point ★.

① ② ③ ④ ⑤ ⑥

Completed.

Doggie | Begin with **Shawl Base** (p. 14).

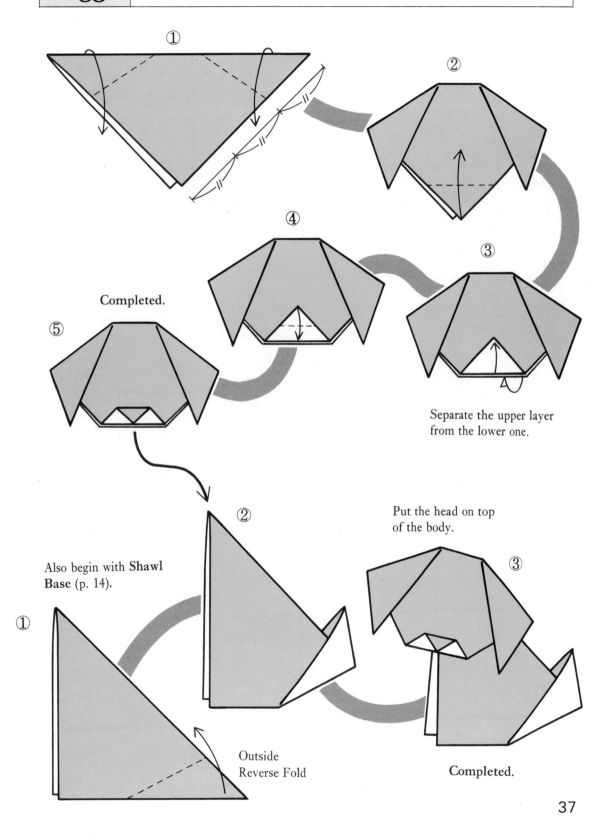

① ② ③

Separate the upper layer
from the lower one.

④

Completed.

⑤

Put the head on top
of the body.

Also begin with **Shawl
Base** (p. 14).

① ② ③

Outside
Reverse Fold

Completed.

Lantern

Begin with **Leaf-Door Base** (p. 13). (Japanese traditional)

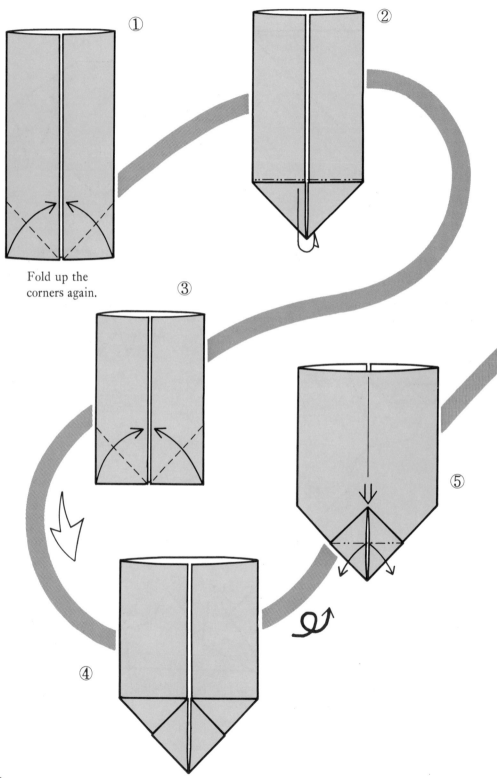

①

②

Fold up the corners again.

③

④

⑤

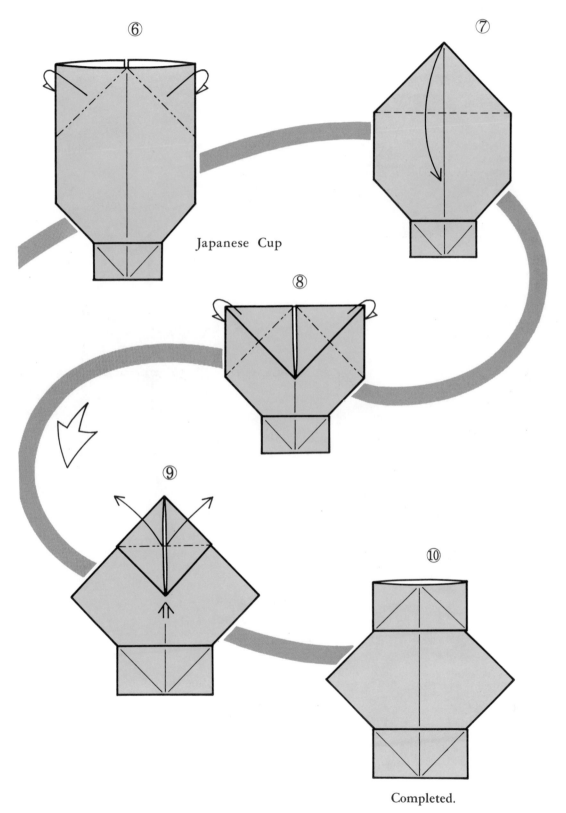

⑥

⑦

Japanese Cup

⑧

⑨

⑩

Completed.

Sailing Boat | Begin with Double-Boat Base (p. 24).

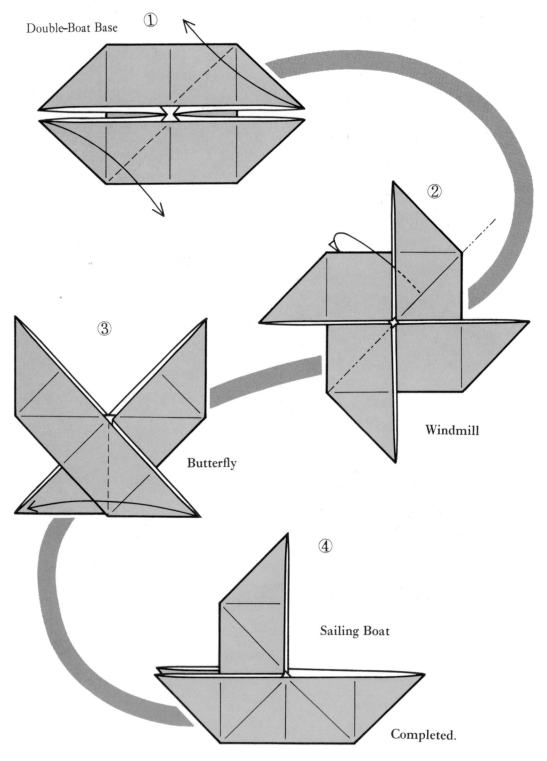

Double-Boat Base ①

②

Windmill

③

Butterfly

④

Sailing Boat

Completed.

Samurai Helmet

Begin with **Helmet Base** (p. 15). (Japanese traditional)

① Fold both flaps up.

② Fold two points outside.

③ Fold up upper flap only.

④ Fold this flap up.

⑤ Fold this flap up on the other side.

⑥ Completed.

Organ

Begin with **Organ Base** (p. 19).

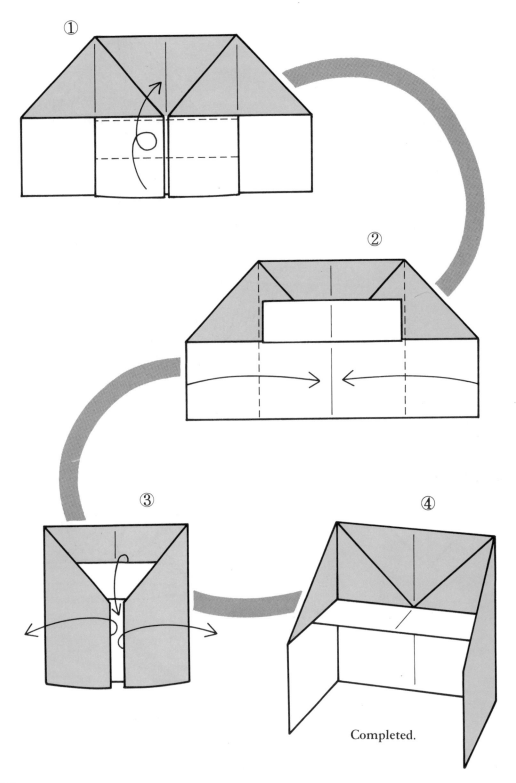

Completed.

Houses

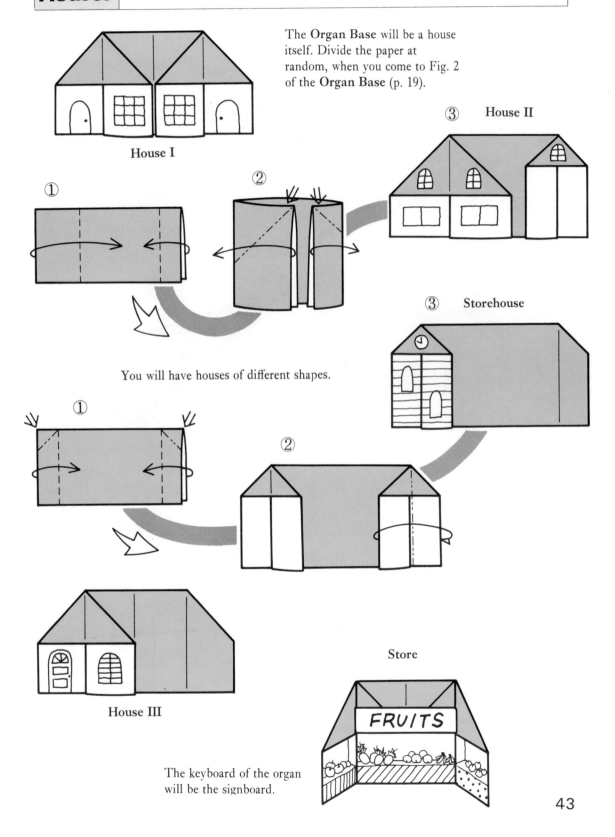

The **Organ Base** will be a house itself. Divide the paper at random, when you come to Fig. 2 of the **Organ Base** (p. 19).

House I

③ House II

① ②

You will have houses of different shapes.

③ Storehouse

① ②

House III

Store

The keyboard of the organ will be the signboard.

FRUITS

Pecking Crow | Begin with **Kite Base** (p. 16). | (Japanese traditional)

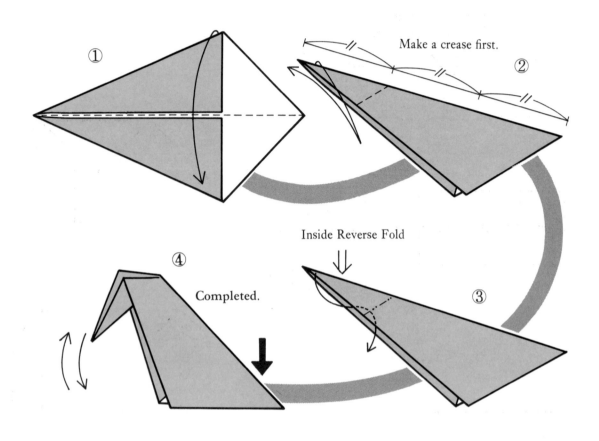

①

② Make a crease first.

Inside Reverse Fold

③

④ Completed.

Happy Coat

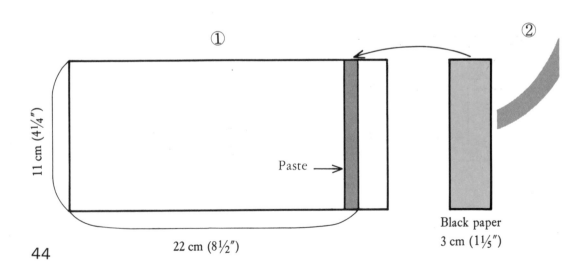

① 11 cm (4¼″) Paste → 22 cm (8½″)

② Black paper 3 cm (1⅕″)

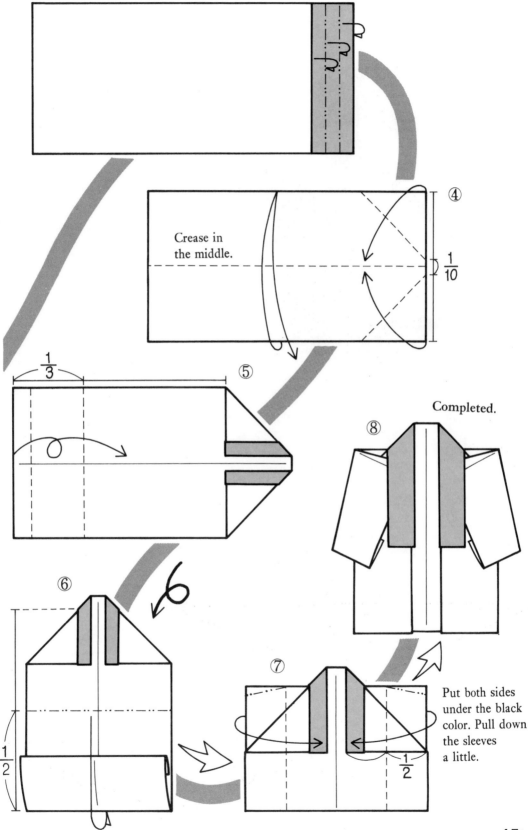

③

④ Crease in the middle.

$\frac{1}{10}$

⑤ $\frac{1}{3}$

⑥ $\frac{1}{2}$

⑦ $\frac{1}{2}$

⑧ Completed.

Put both sides under the black color. Pull down the sleeves a little.

45

Monkey | Begin with **Diamond Base** (p. 17).

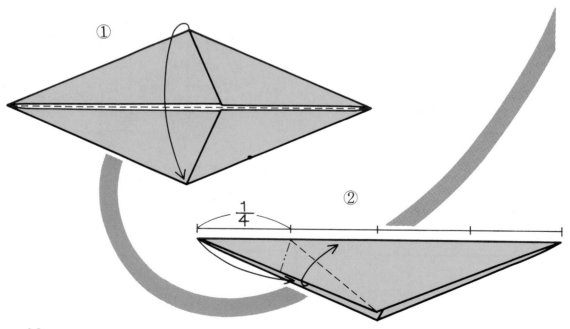

① ②

$\frac{1}{4}$

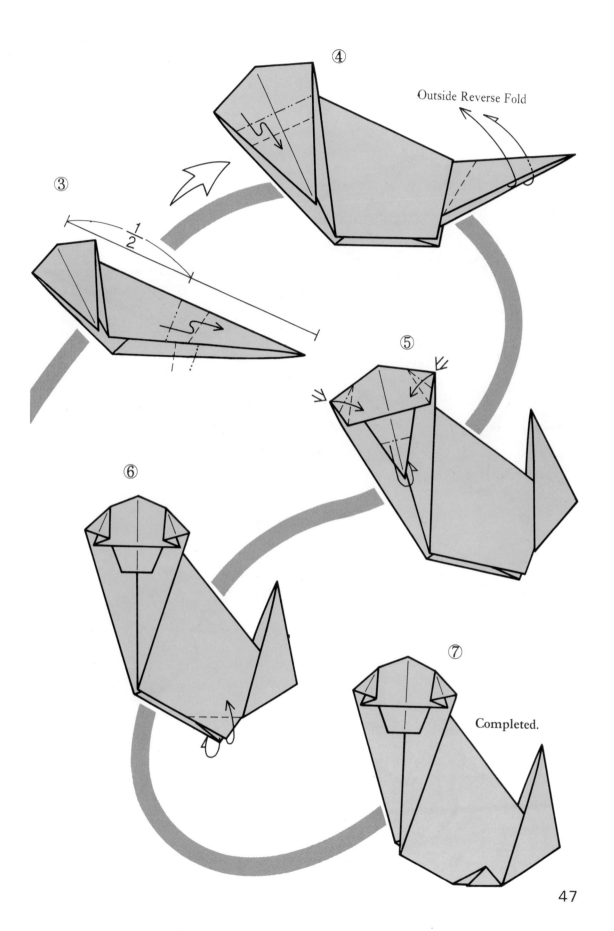

③

$\dfrac{1}{2}$

④

Outside Reverse Fold

⑤

⑥

⑦

Completed.

47

Rocking Pigeon Begin with **Fish Base** (p. 23).

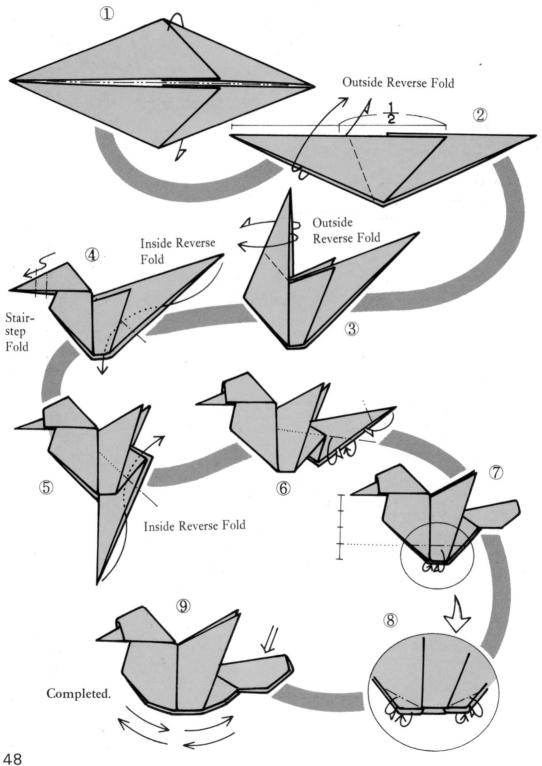

①

Outside Reverse Fold

$\frac{1}{2}$

②

Outside Reverse Fold

③

Inside Reverse Fold

④

Stair-step Fold

⑤

Inside Reverse Fold

⑥

⑦

⑧

⑨

Completed.

Fox
Begin with **Shawl Base** (p. 14).   (by Mitsuo Okuda)

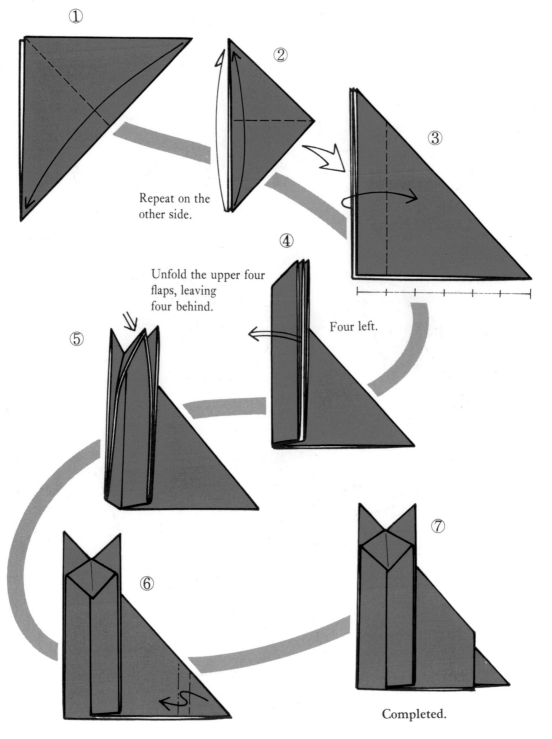

①

②

Repeat on the
other side.

③

④

Unfold the upper four
flaps, leaving
four behind.

Four left.

⑤

⑥

⑦

Completed.

Barking Dog

Begin with **Shawl Base** (p. 14).

(by Paul Jackson)

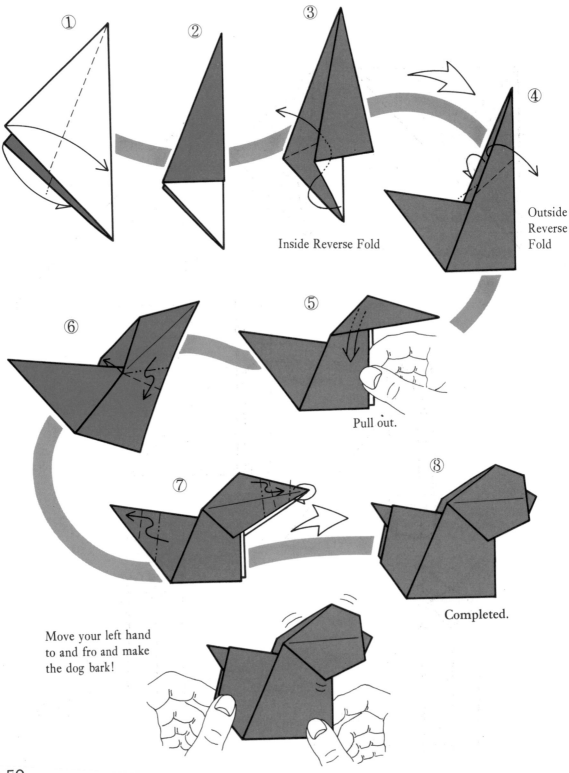

Inside Reverse Fold

Outside Reverse Fold

Pull out.

Move your left hand to and fro and make the dog bark!

Completed.

Heart Begin with **Book Base** (p. 12). (by Hiroshi Kumasaka)

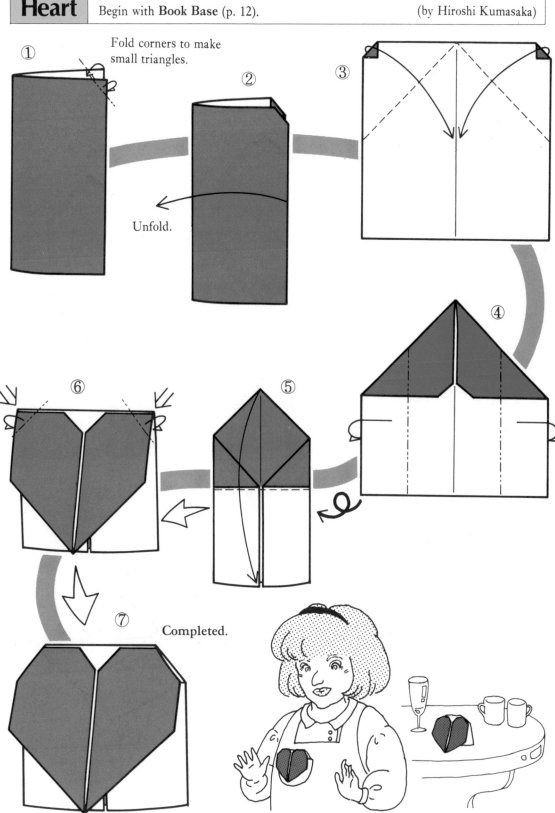

① Fold corners to make small triangles.

② Unfold.

③

④

⑤

⑥

⑦ Completed.

Flower

Begin with **Square Base** (p. 20).

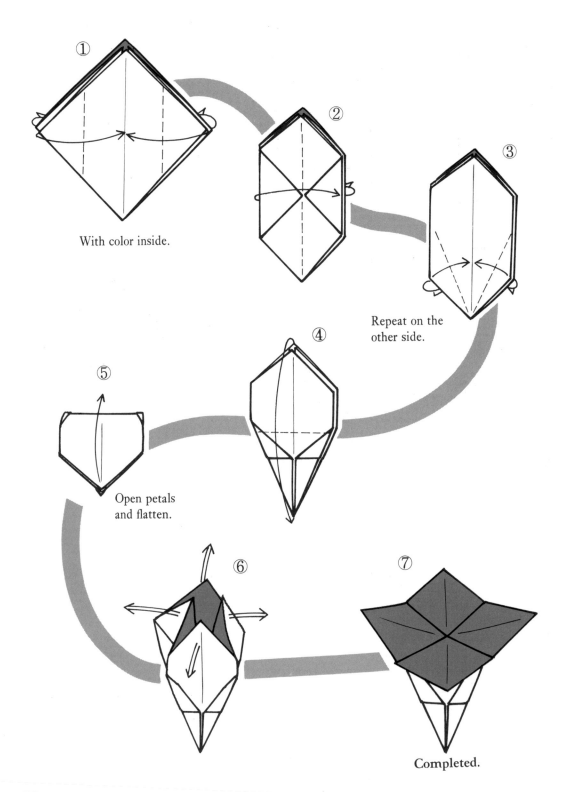

① With color inside.

②

③ Repeat on the other side.

④

⑤ Open petals and flatten.

⑥

⑦ Completed.

Tree

Begin with **Kite Base** (p. 16). (by the late Mr. Robert Harbin)

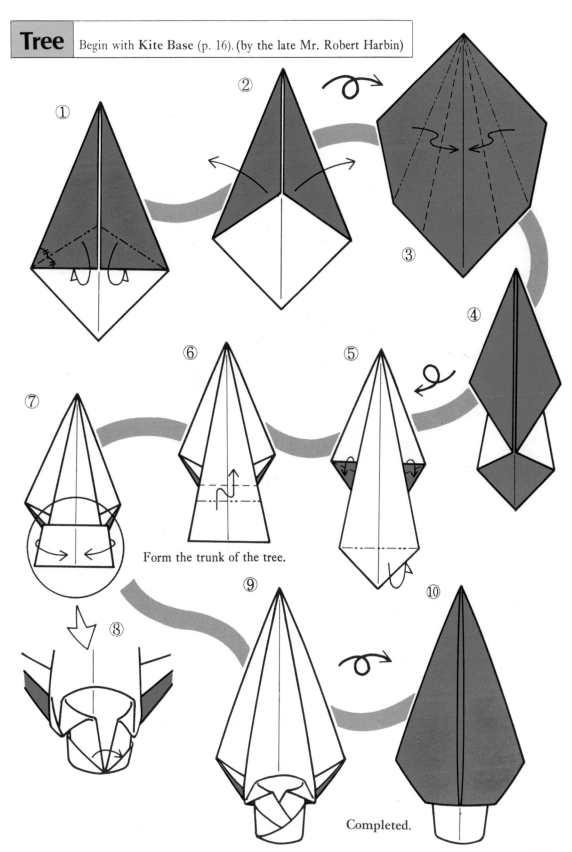

Form the trunk of the tree.

Completed.

Fish

Begin wish **Fish Base** (p. 23).

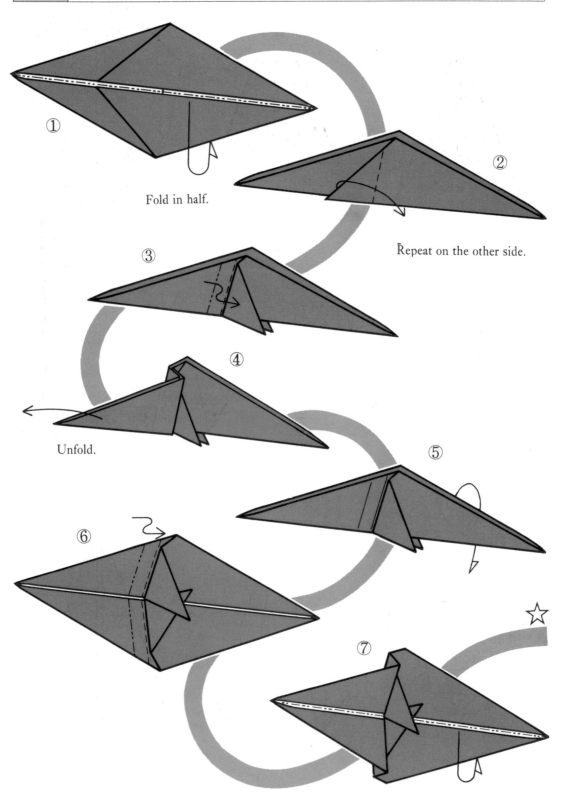

① Fold in half.

② Repeat on the other side.

③

④ Unfold.

⑤

⑥

⑦ ☆

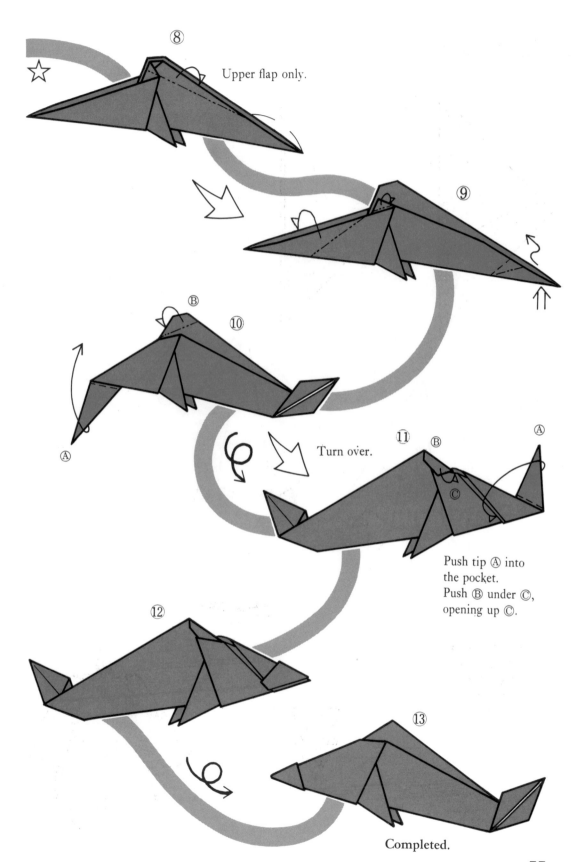

⑧ Upper flap only.

⑨

⑩

Ⓐ

Ⓑ

Turn over.

⑪ Ⓑ Ⓐ
Ⓒ

Push tip Ⓐ into
the pocket.
Push Ⓑ under Ⓒ,
opening up Ⓒ.

⑫

⑬

Completed.

Grape Leaf

Begin with **Shawl Base** (p. 14). (Hint from Alice Gray's Leaf)

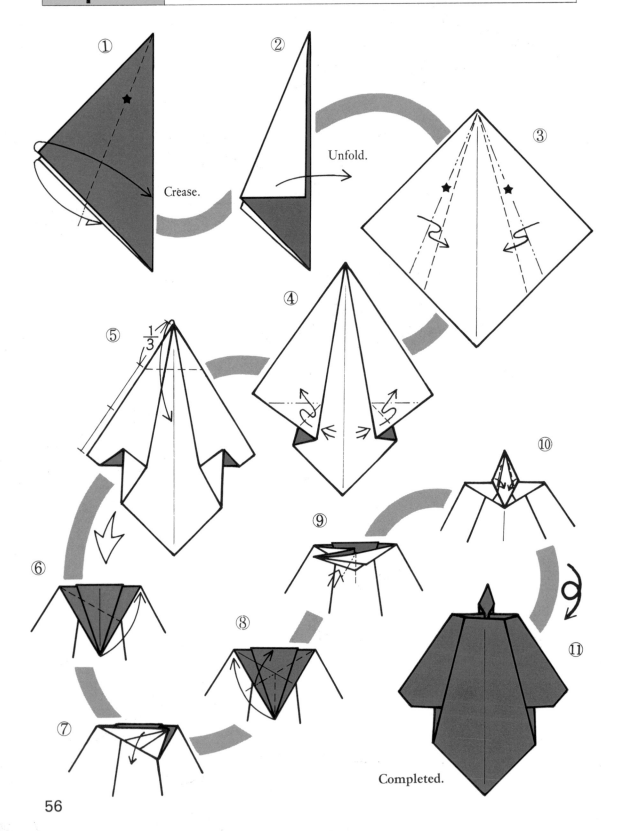

① Crease.

② Unfold.

③

④

⑤ 1/3

⑥

⑦

⑧

⑨

⑩

⑪

Completed.

Balloon

Grape Leaf

Fox

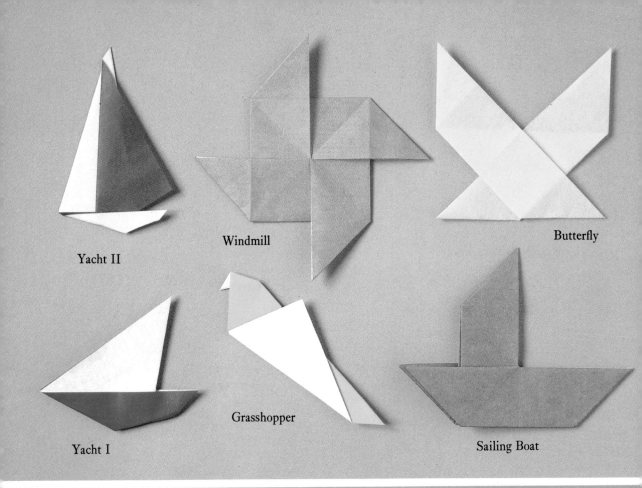

Yacht II

Windmill

Butterfly

Yacht I

Grasshopper

Sailing Boat

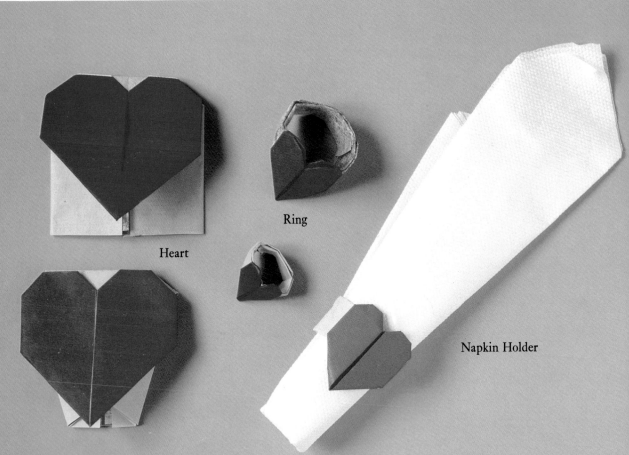

Heart

Ring

Napkin Holder

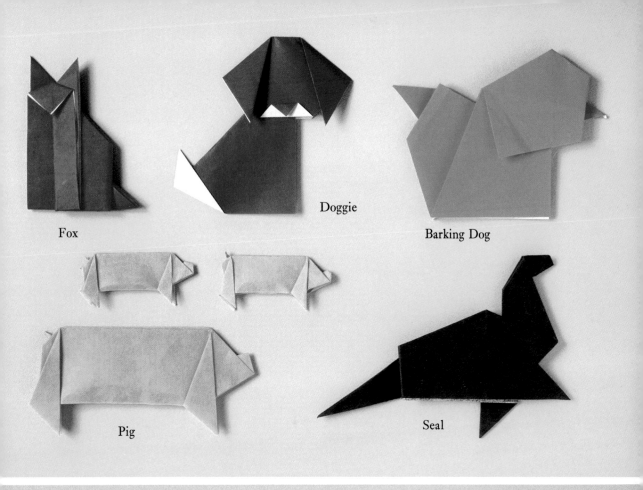

Fox

Doggie

Barking Dog

Pig

Seal

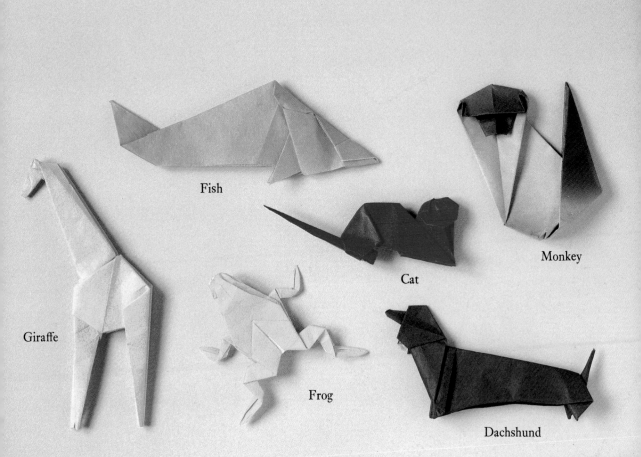

Fish

Monkey

Giraffe

Cat

Frog

Dachshund

Organ

Cup

Samurai Helmet

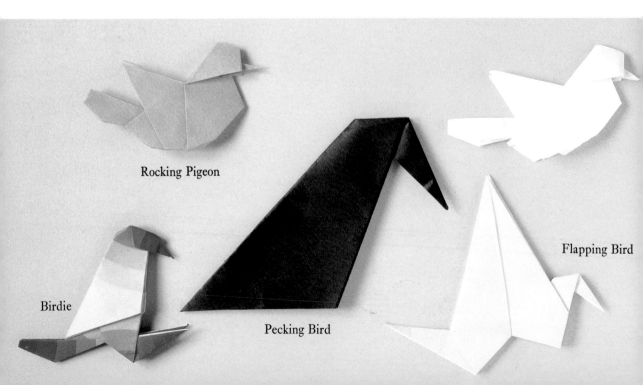

Rocking Pigeon

Birdie

Pecking Bird

Flapping Bird

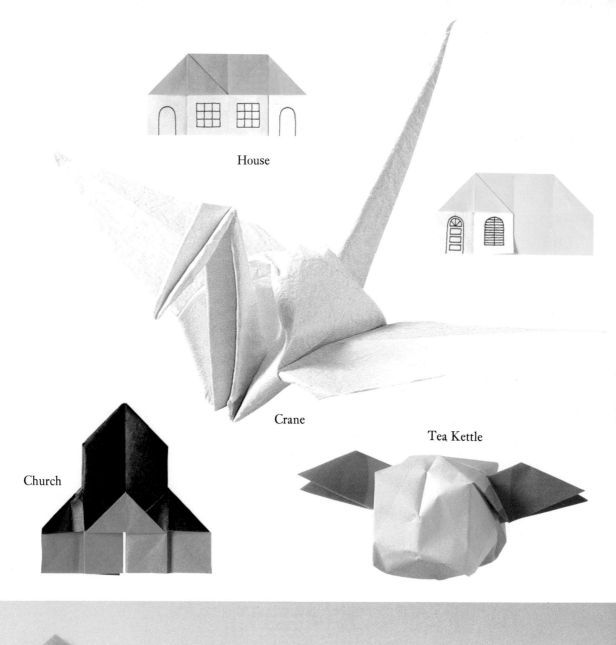

House

Crane

Tea Kettle

Church

Jet Plane

Motorboat

61

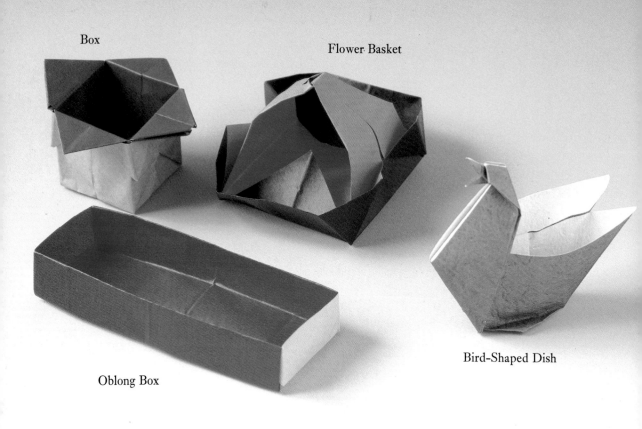

Box

Flower Basket

Bird-Shaped Dish

Oblong Box

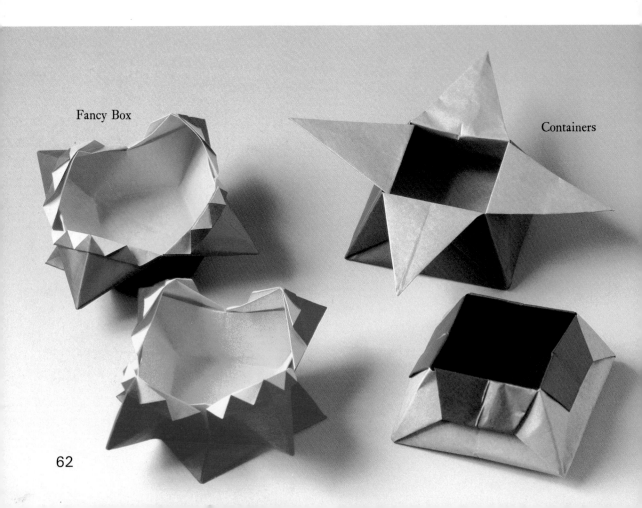

Fancy Box

Containers

62

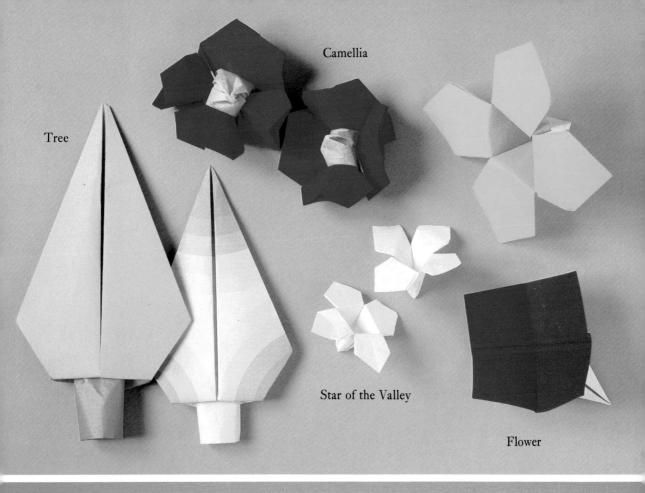

Tree

Camellia

Star of the Valley

Flower

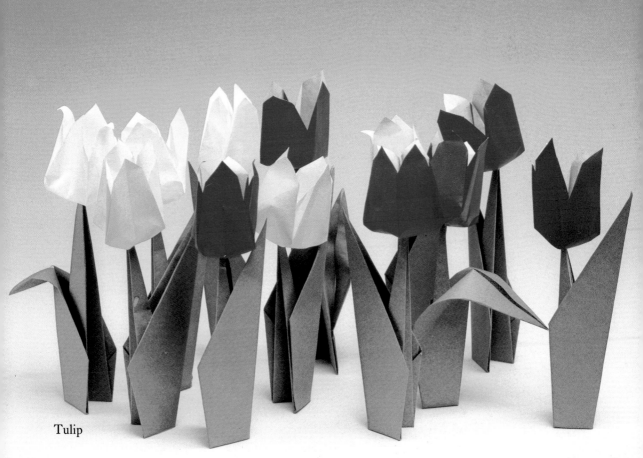

Tulip

Star

Lantern

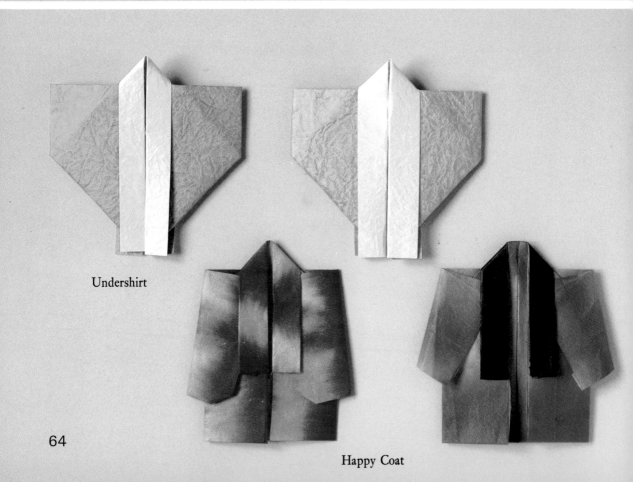

Undershirt

64

Happy Coat

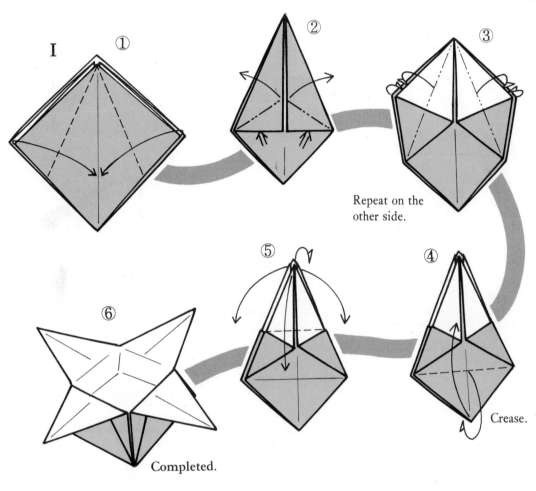

I ① ② ③

Repeat on the other side.

⑥ ⑤ ④

Completed. Crease.

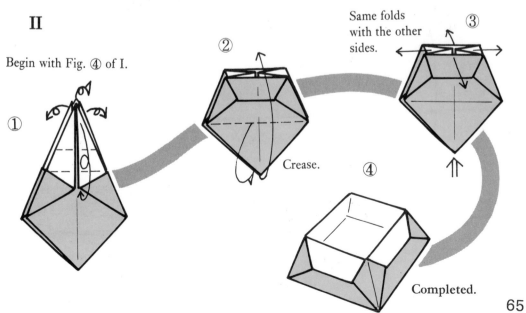

II

Begin with Fig. ④ of I.

① ② ③

Same folds with the other sides.

Crease. ④

Completed.

65

Motorboat

Begin with **Leaf-Door Base** (p. 13).   (Japanese traditional)

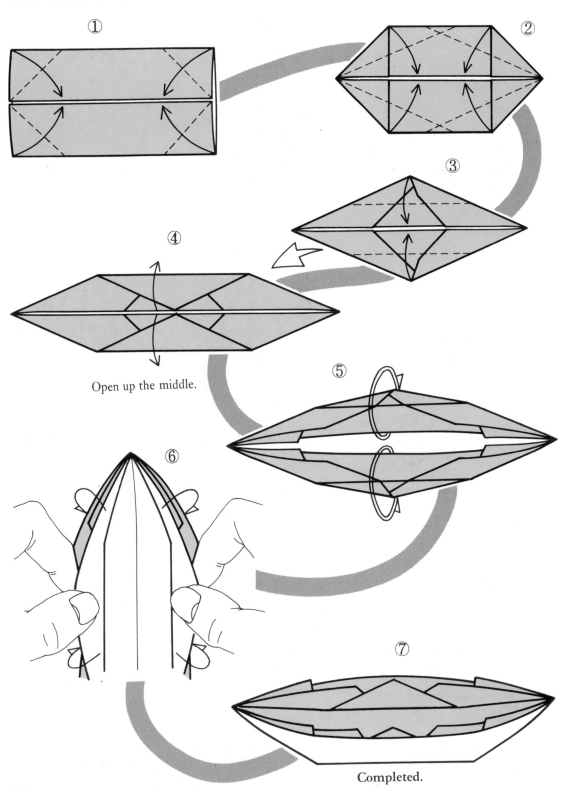

Open up the middle.

Completed.

Jet Plane

Begin with **Leaf-Door Base** (p. 13).

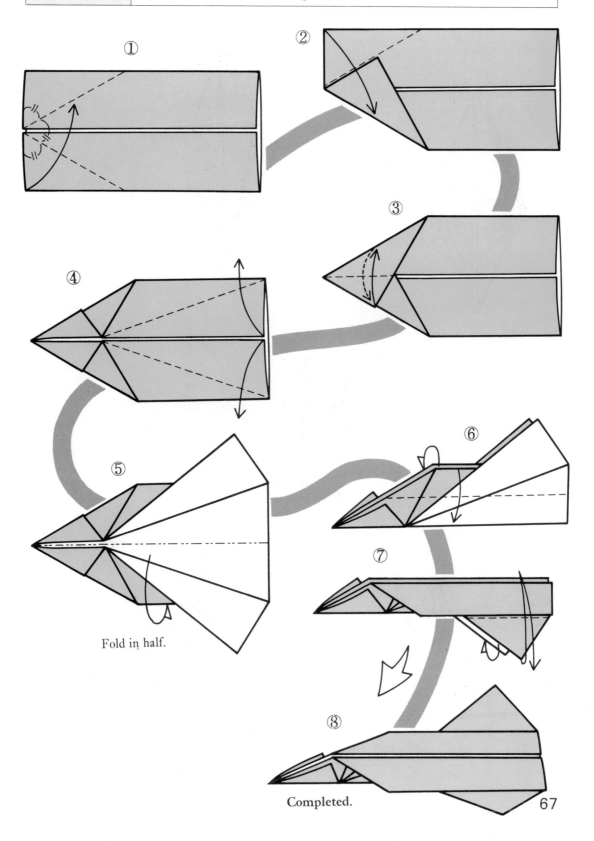

① ② ③ ④

⑤ Fold in half.

⑥ ⑦

⑧ Completed.

Crane

Begin with **Bird Base** (p. 22).   (Japanese traditional)

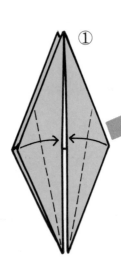

①

Same fold on the other side.

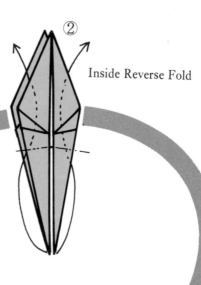

②

Inside Reverse Fold

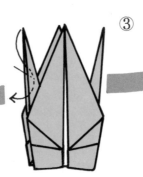

③

④

Blow in, pulling the wings to both sides.

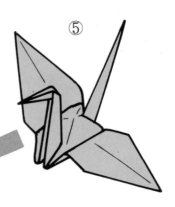

⑤

Flapping Bird   Begin with **Bird Base** (p. 22).

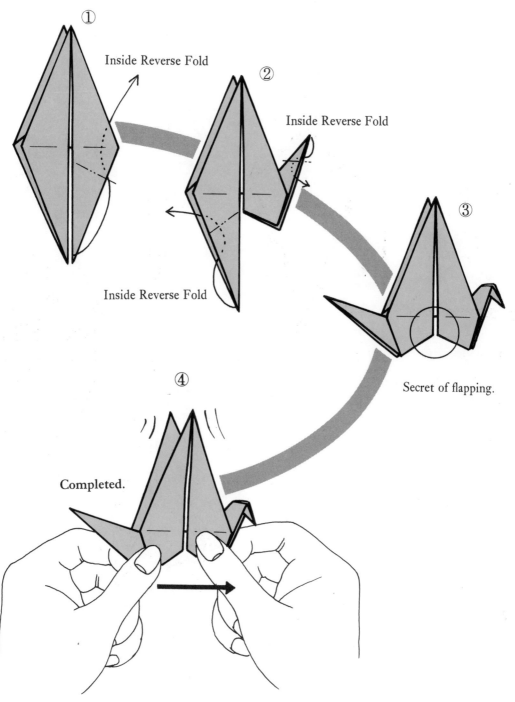

① Inside Reverse Fold

② Inside Reverse Fold

Inside Reverse Fold

③

Secret of flapping.

④ Completed.

Holding the lower part of the tail with your left hand, pull the lower part of the neck quickly with your right hand. The wings will flap lightly.

Camellia

Begin with **Bird Base** (p. 22).

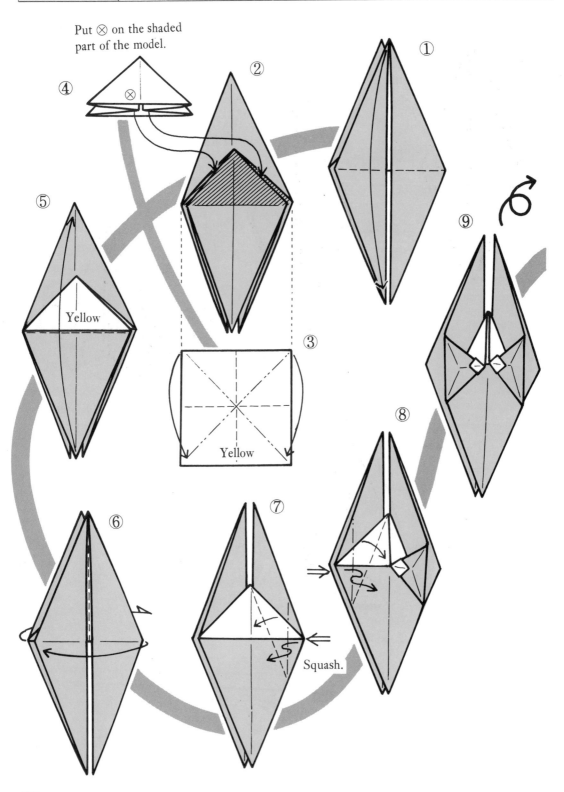

Put ⊗ on the shaded part of the model.

④

②

①

⑤

Yellow

③

Yellow

⑨

⑧

⑥

⑦

Squash.

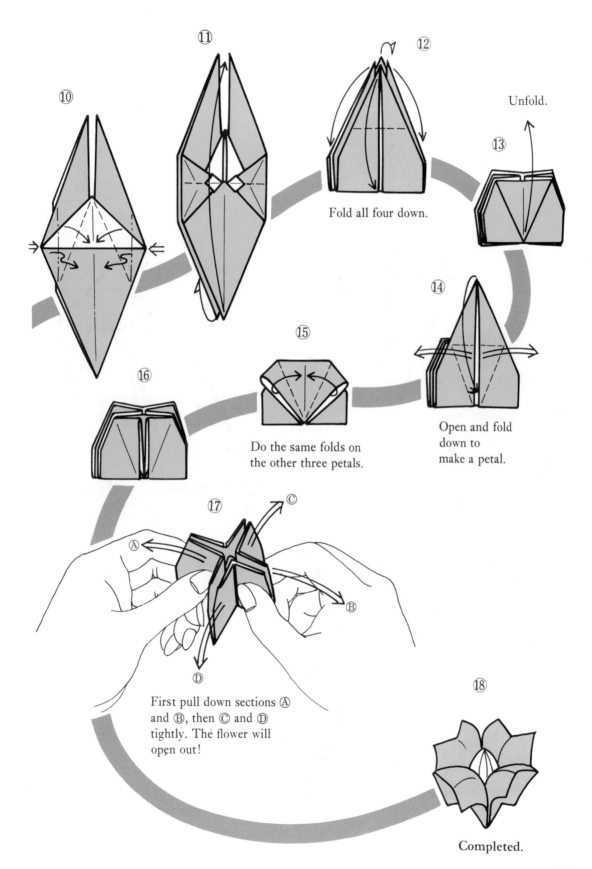

⑩

⑪

⑫

Fold all four down.

Unfold.

⑬

⑭

Open and fold
down to
make a petal.

⑮

Do the same folds on
the other three petals.

⑯

⑰

Ⓒ

Ⓐ

Ⓑ

Ⓓ

First pull down sections Ⓐ
and Ⓑ, then Ⓒ and Ⓓ
tightly. The flower will
open out!

⑱

Completed.

71

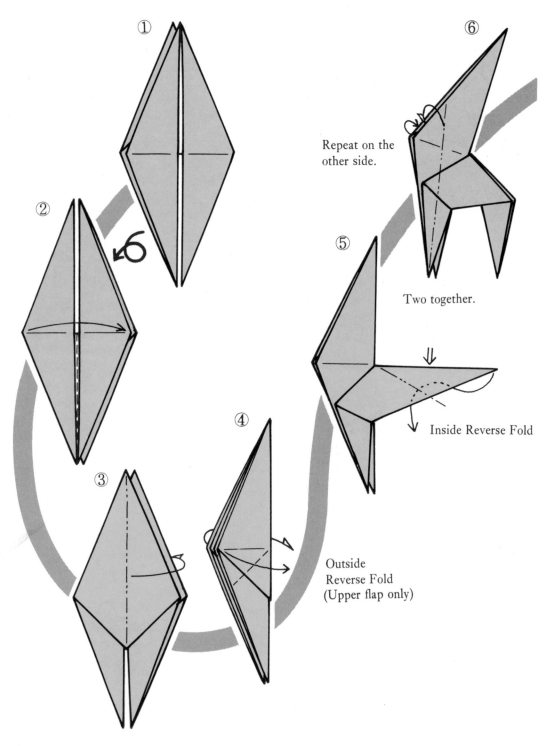

①

②

③

④ Outside
Reverse Fold
(Upper flap only)

⑤ Two together.

⇓

Inside Reverse Fold

⑥ Repeat on the
other side.

72

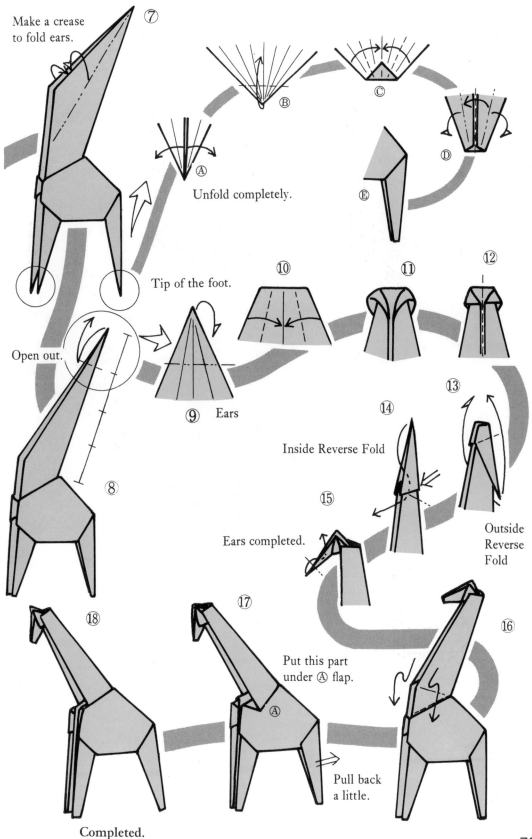

⑦ Make a crease to fold ears.

Ⓐ Unfold completely.

Ⓑ

Ⓒ

Ⓓ

Ⓔ

Open out.

⑧

Tip of the foot.

⑨ Ears

⑩

⑪

⑫

⑬

⑭ Inside Reverse Fold

Outside Reverse Fold

⑮ Ears completed.

⑯ Put this part under Ⓐ flap.

⑰

Ⓐ

Pull back a little.

⑱

Completed.

73

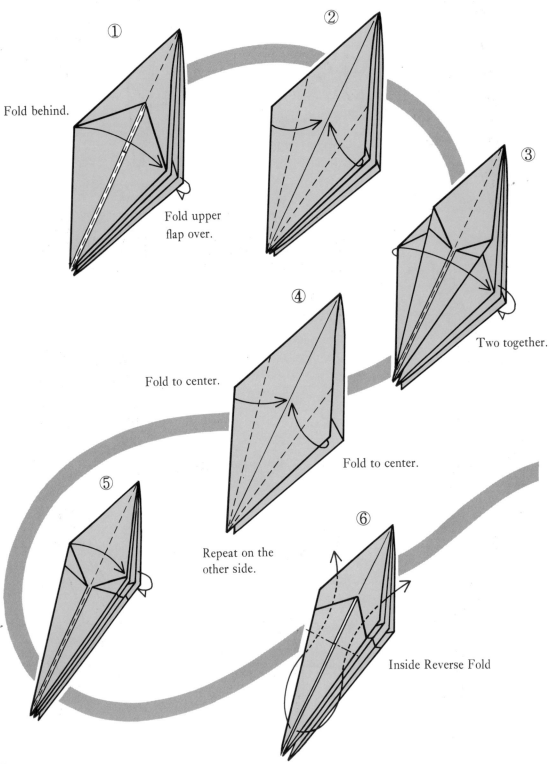

① Fold behind.

Fold upper flap over.

②

③ Two together.

④ Fold to center.

Fold to center.

⑤ Repeat on the other side.

⑥ Inside Reverse Fold

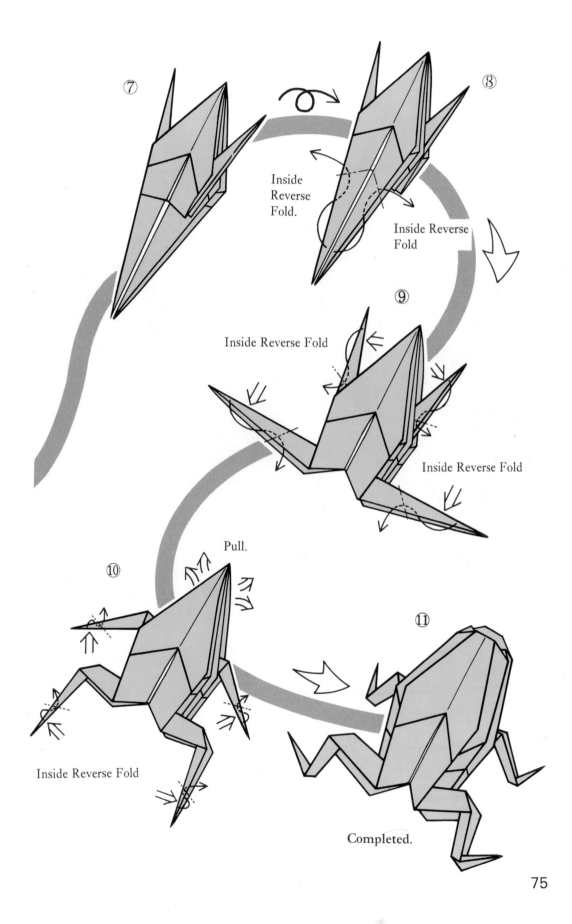

⑦

⑧

Inside
Reverse
Fold.

Inside Reverse
Fold

⑨

Inside Reverse Fold

Inside Reverse Fold

Pull.

⑩

Inside Reverse Fold

⑪

Completed.

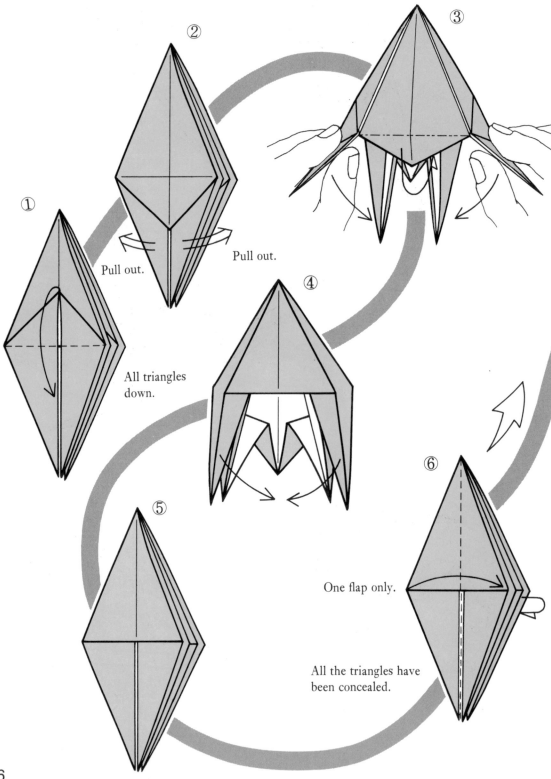

①

② Pull out.   Pull out.

All triangles
down.

③

④

⑤

⑥ One flap only.

All the triangles have
been concealed.

⑦

⑧

Do the same folds with the other three flaps by pulling out two legs to both sides.

⑨

Repeat on the other side.

⑩

Curl petals.

⑪

Completed.

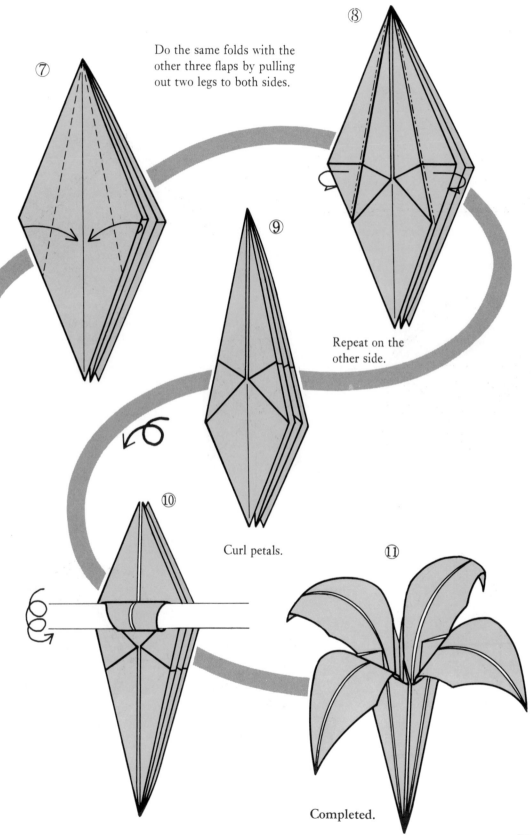

Balloon | Begin with **Water-Bomb Base** (p. 21). (Japanese traditional)

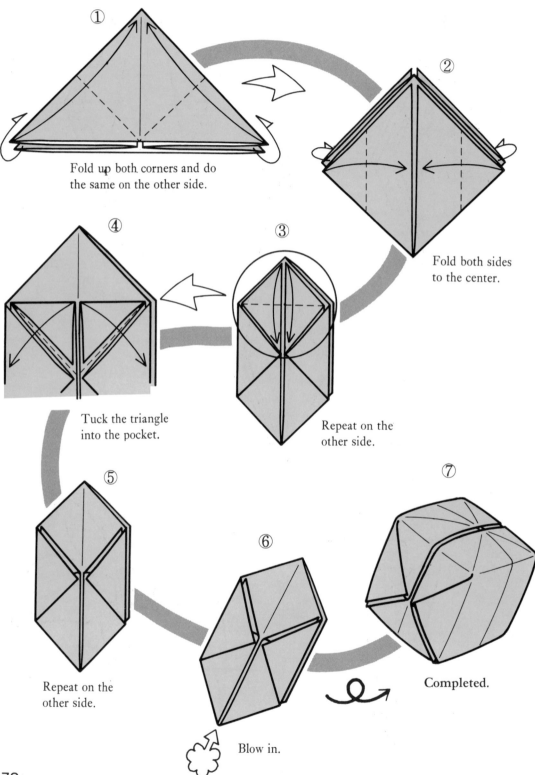

① Fold up both corners and do the same on the other side.

② Fold both sides to the center.

③ Repeat on the other side.

④ Tuck the triangle into the pocket.

⑤ Repeat on the other side.

⑥ Blow in.

⑦ Completed.

Bird-Shaped Dish   Begin with **Fish Base** (p. 23).

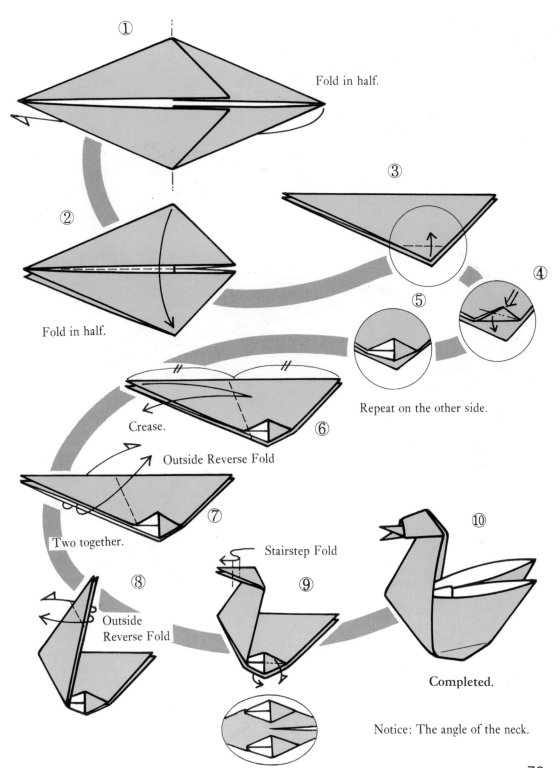

① Fold in half.

② Fold in half.

③

④

⑤ Repeat on the other side.

⑥ Crease.   Outside Reverse Fold

⑦ Two together.

⑧ Outside Reverse Fold

⑨ Stairstep Fold

⑩ Completed.

Notice: The angle of the neck.

Seal Begin with **Fish Base** (p. 23).

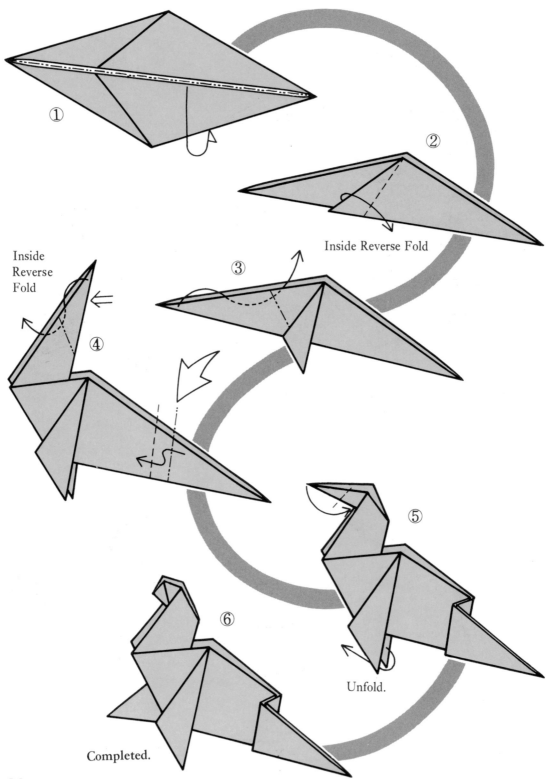

①

② Inside Reverse Fold

③

Inside Reverse Fold

④

⑤

Unfold.

⑥

Completed.

Church

Begin with **Water-Bomb Base** (p. 21).

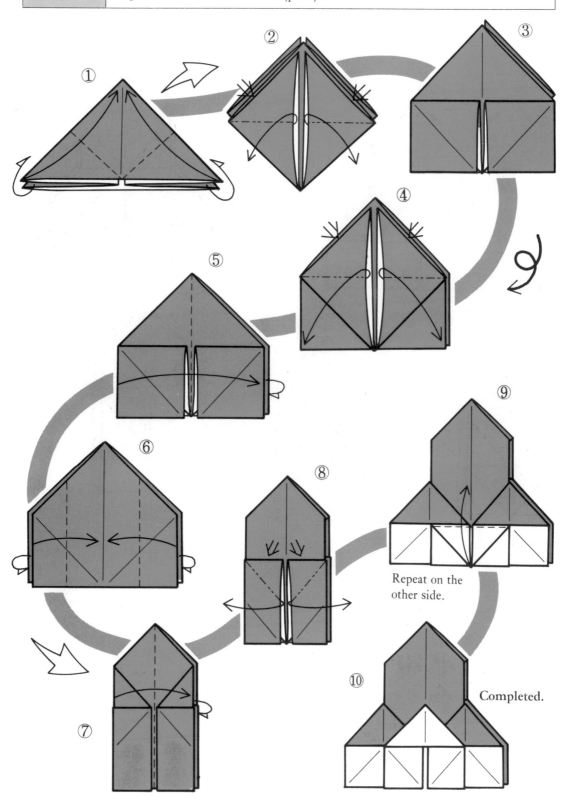

Repeat on the other side.

Completed.

Box

Begin with **Church** (p. 81). (by George Cooper)

Let us make a box from the church we have just folded.

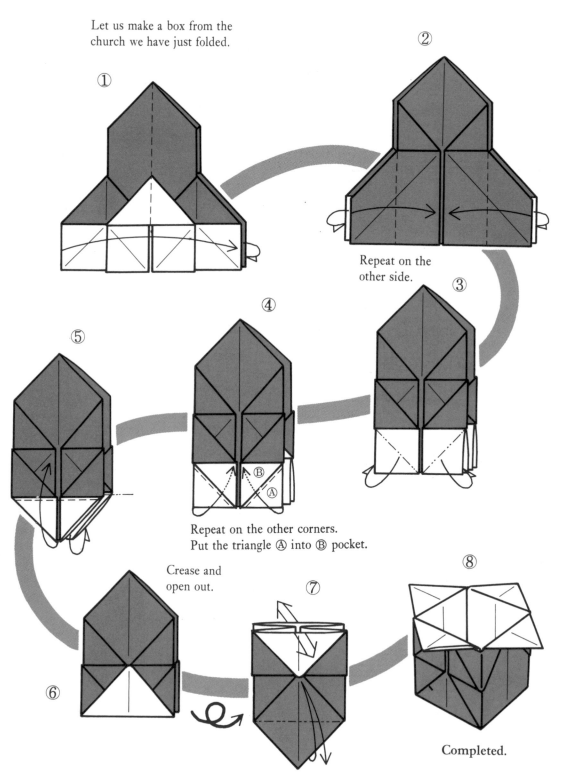

① ②

Repeat on the other side.

③

④

Repeat on the other corners.
Put the triangle Ⓐ into Ⓑ pocket.

⑤

Crease and
open out.

⑥ ⑦ ⑧

Completed.

Oblong Box

Begin with **Organ Base** (p. 19).

(by Hideaki Sakata)

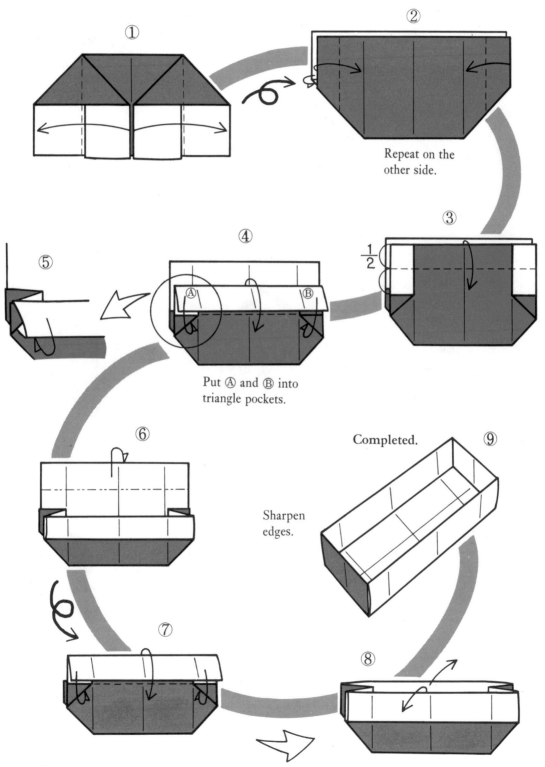

①

② Repeat on the other side.

③ $\frac{1}{2}$

④ Put Ⓐ and Ⓑ into triangle pockets.

⑤

⑥

⑦

⑧

⑨ Completed.

Sharpen edges.

Star of the Valley

Begin with **Square Base** (p. 20).

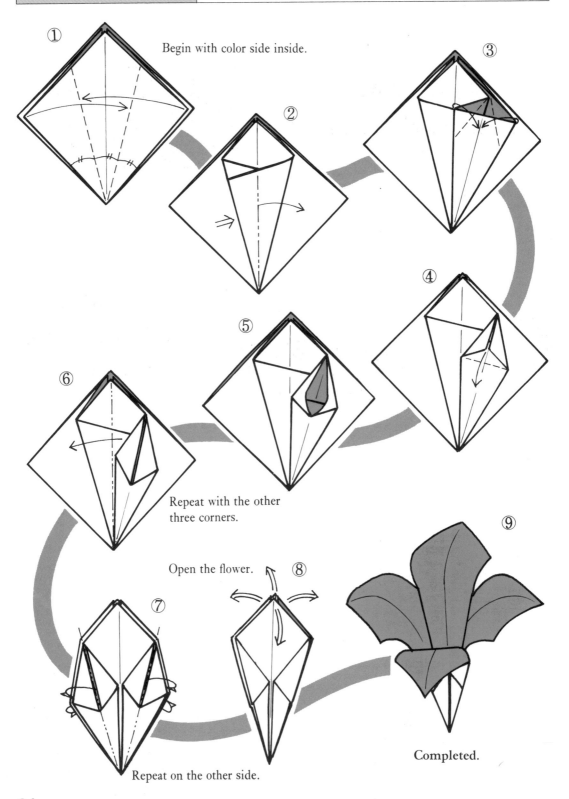

① Begin with color side inside.

②

③

④

⑤

⑥ Repeat with the other three corners.

⑦ Repeat on the other side.

Open the flower. ⑧

⑨ Completed.

Tea Kettle
Begin with **Water-Bomb Base** (p. 21).

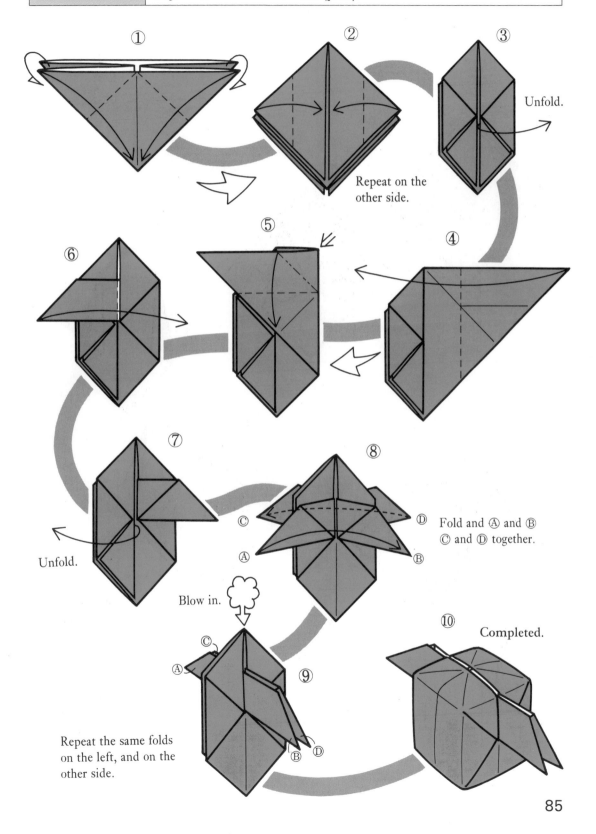

①

② Repeat on the other side.

③ Unfold.

④

⑤

⑥

⑦ Unfold.

⑧ Fold and Ⓐ and Ⓑ Ⓒ and Ⓓ together.

Ⓒ Ⓐ Ⓓ Ⓑ

Blow in.

⑨ Ⓒ Ⓐ Ⓑ Ⓓ

Repeat the same folds on the left, and on the other side.

⑩ Completed.

Tulip Begin with **Square Base** (p. 20).

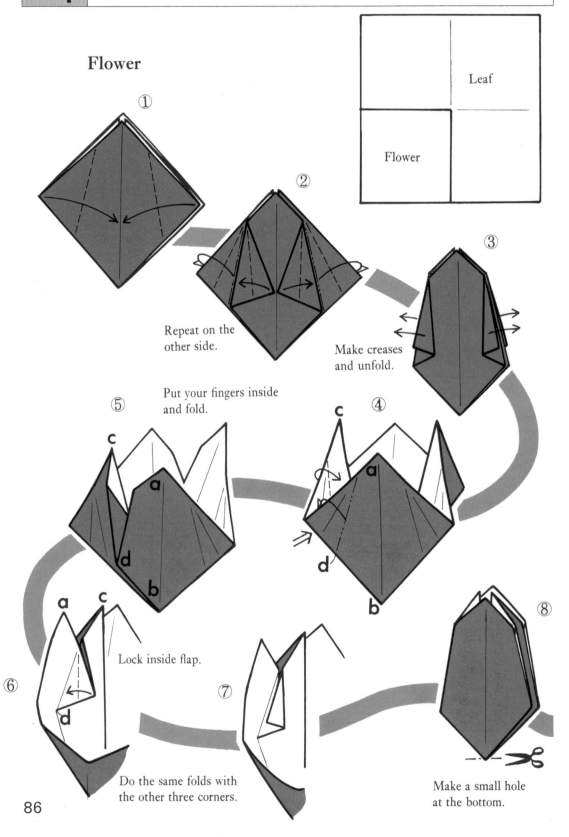

Flower

①

② Repeat on the other side.

③ Make creases and unfold.

Leaf

Flower

④

⑤ Put your fingers inside and fold.

⑥ Lock inside flap.

⑦ Do the same folds with the other three corners.

⑧ Make a small hole at the bottom.

86

Leaf Begin with **Diamond Base** (p. 17).

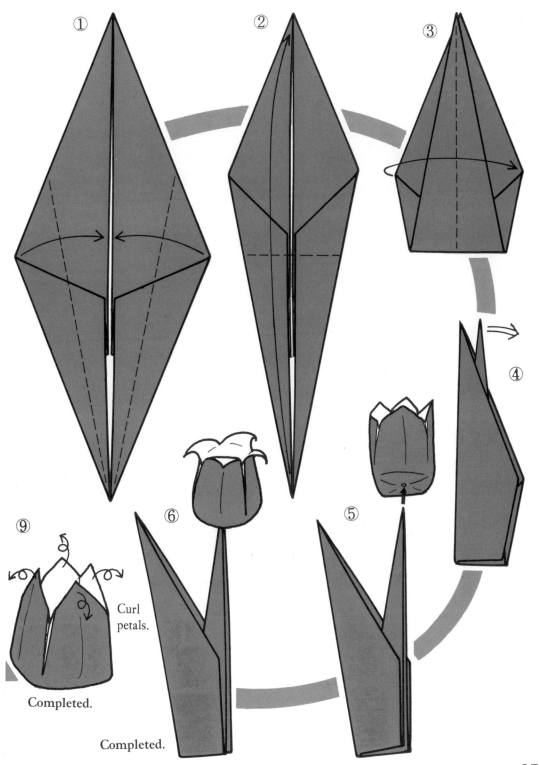

① ② ③ ④ ⑤ ⑥

⑨ Curl petals.

Completed.

Completed.

Fancy Box — Begin with **Blintz Base** (p. 18).

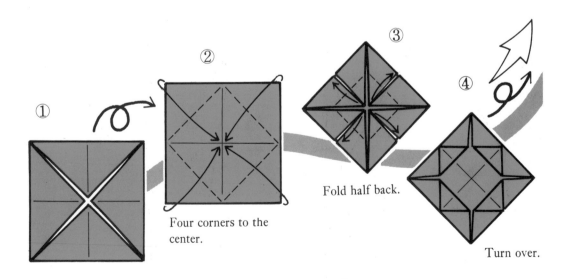

① ②

Four corners to the center.

③

Fold half back.

④

Turn over.

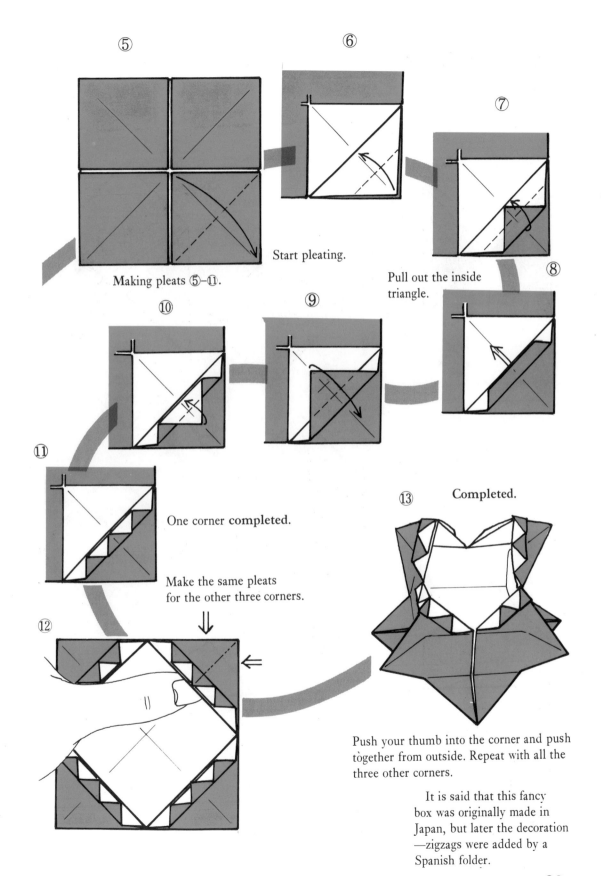

⑤

Making pleats ⑤–⑪.

⑥

Start pleating.

⑦

Pull out the inside triangle.

⑧

⑩

⑨

⑪

One corner **completed**.

Make the same pleats for the other three corners.

⇓

⑫

⑬ Completed.

Push your thumb into the corner and push together from outside. Repeat with all the three other corners.

It is said that this fancy box was originally made in Japan, but later the decoration —zigzags were added by a Spanish folder.

89

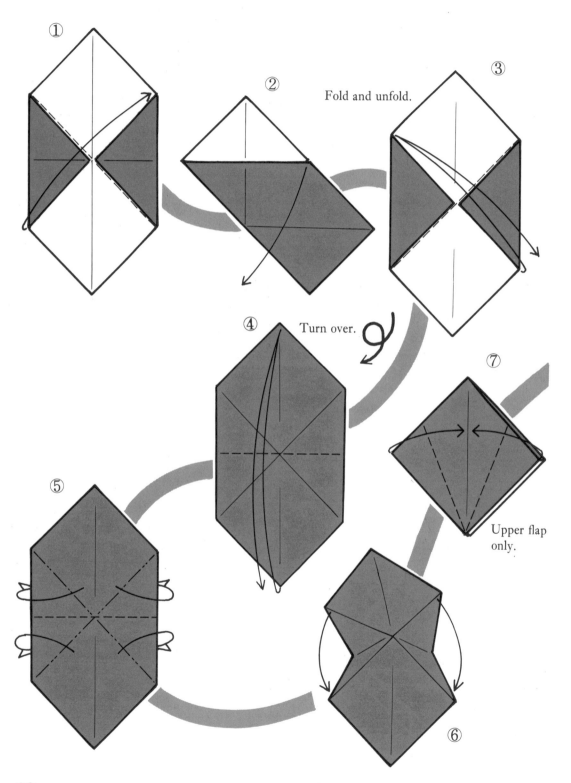

①

② Fold and unfold.

③

④ Turn over.

⑤

⑥

⑦ Upper flap only.

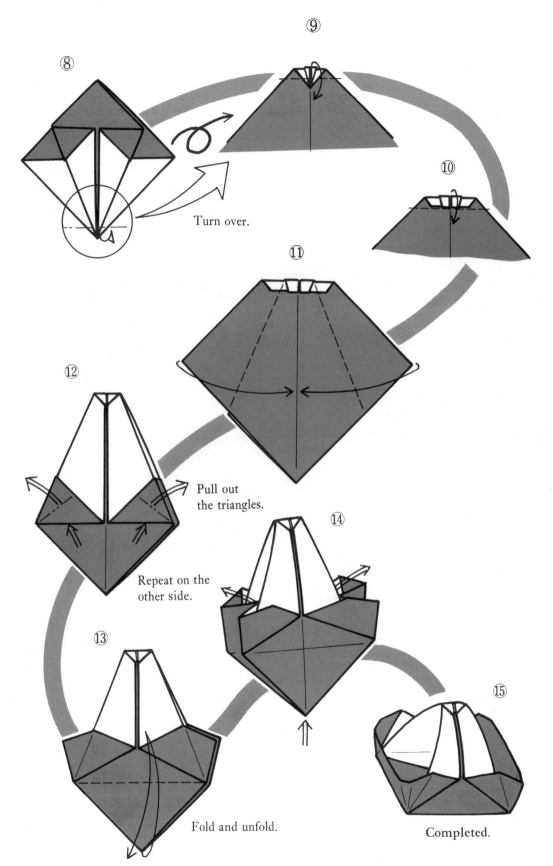

⑧

⑨

⑩

⑪

⑫

Turn over.

Pull out
the triangles.

Repeat on the
other side.

⑬

⑭

⑮

Fold and unfold.

Completed.

Pig Begin with **Pig Base** (p. 25).

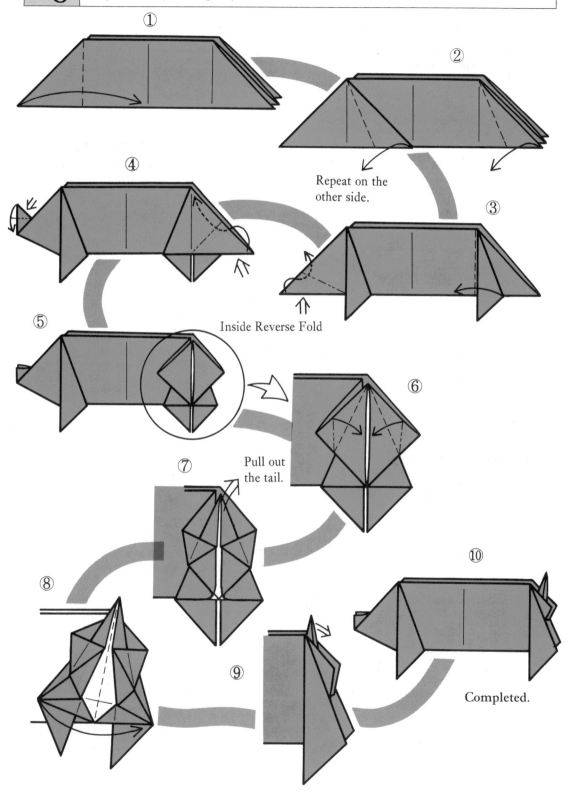

①

②

Repeat on the
other side.

③

④

Inside Reverse Fold

⑤

Pull out
the tail.

⑥

⑦

⑧

⑨

⑩

Completed.

92

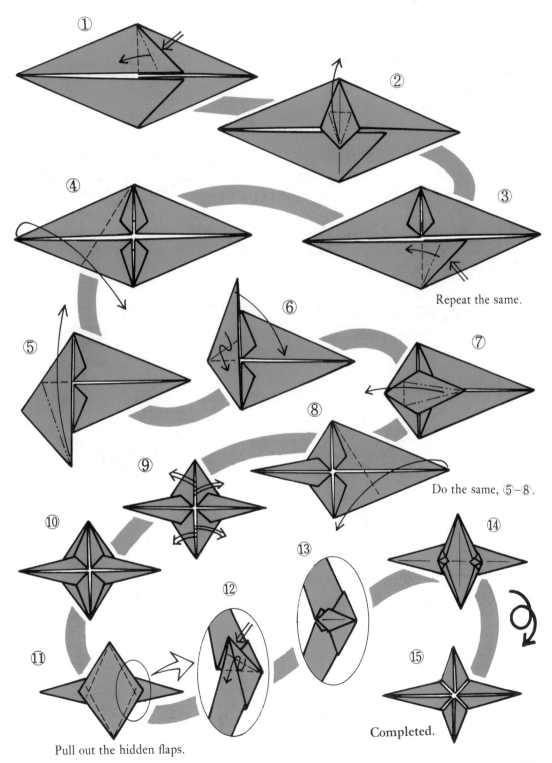

①

②

④

③ Repeat the same.

⑤

⑥

⑦

⑧ Do the same, ⑤–⑧.

⑨

⑩

⑪ Pull out the hidden flaps.

⑫

⑬

⑭

⑮ Completed.

93

Birdie

Begin with **Bird Base** (p. 22).

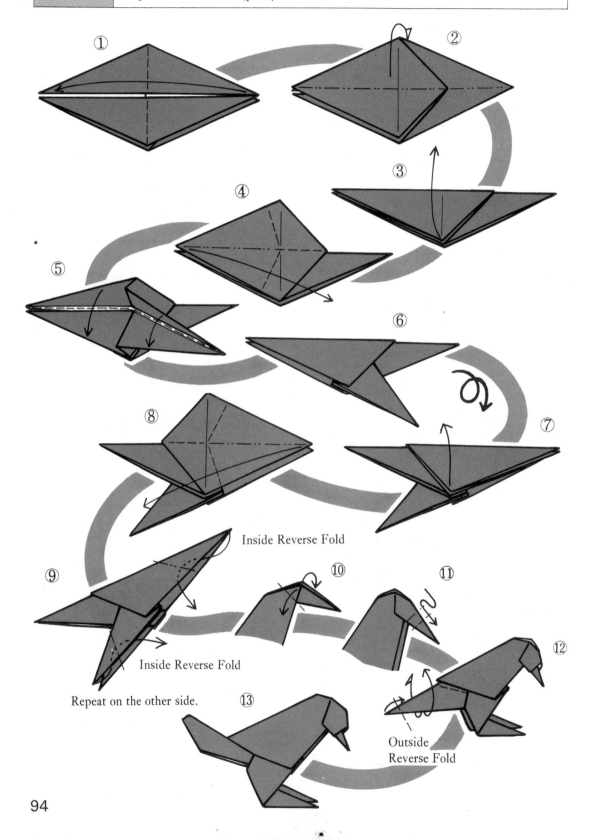

① ②

③ ④

⑤ ⑥

⑦ ⑧

Inside Reverse Fold

⑨

Inside Reverse Fold

Repeat on the other side.

⑩ ⑪ ⑫

Outside
Reverse Fold

⑬

Napkin Holder

Begin with **Book Base** (p. 12).   (by Hiroshi Kumasaka)

①

② Unfold.

③

④

⑤

⑥

⑦

⑧

⑨

⑩

⑪

If you fold this with small paper,
you will have a heart ring.

⑫

⑬

⑭

Completed.

Cat

Begin with **Diamond Base** (p. 17).

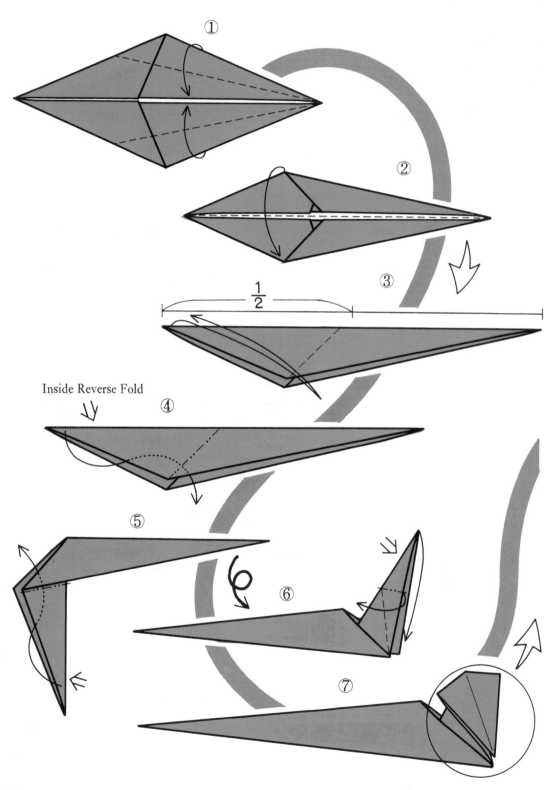

Inside Reverse Fold

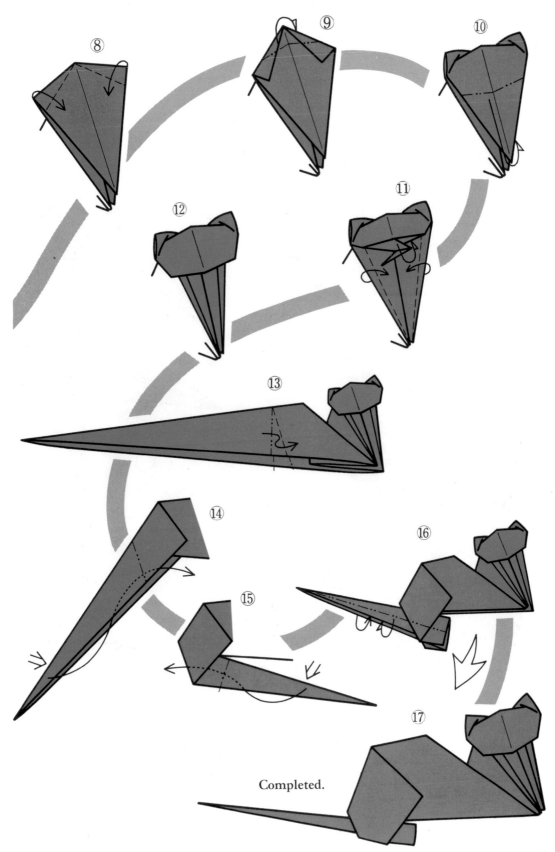

⑧ ⑨ ⑩ ⑪ ⑫ ⑬ ⑭ ⑮ ⑯ ⑰

Completed.

Dachshund

(by Vincente Palacios)

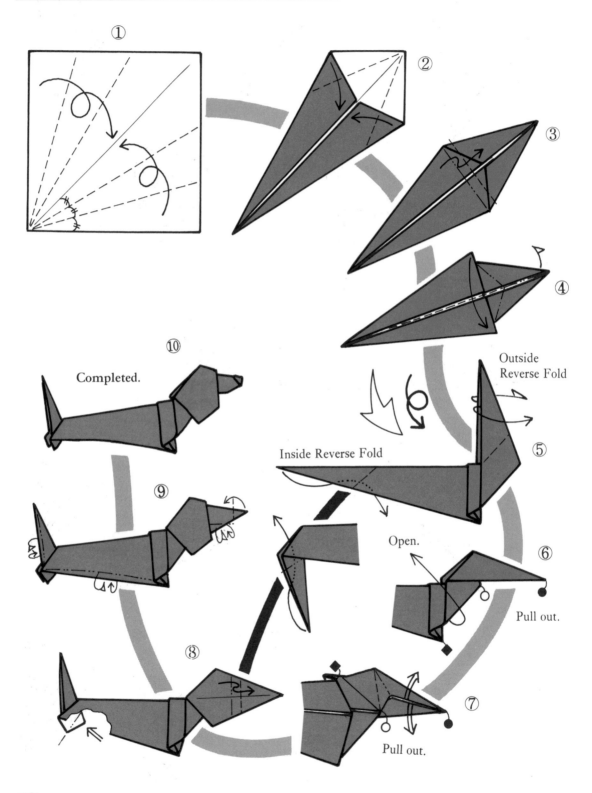

① ② ③ ④

⑤ Outside Reverse Fold

Inside Reverse Fold

Open.

⑥ Pull out.

⑦ Pull out.

⑧

⑨

⑩ Completed.

Coasters | Begin with **Blintz Base** (p. 18).

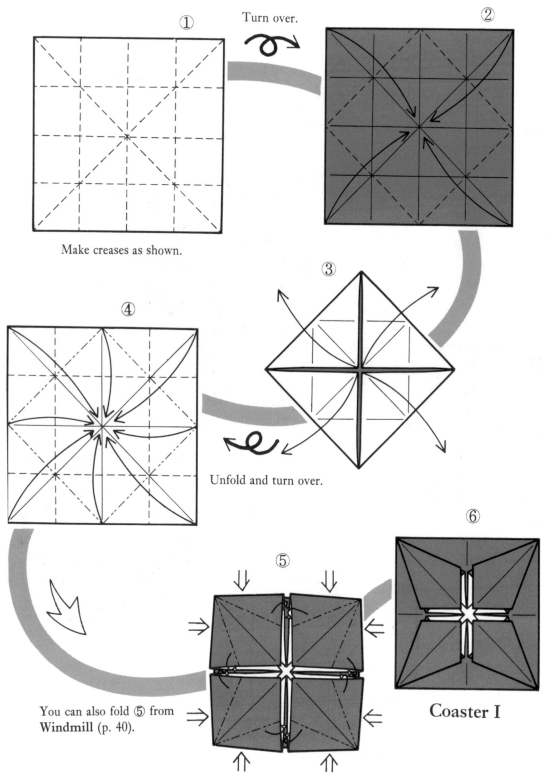

Turn over.

① Make creases as shown.

②

③ Unfold and turn over.

④

⑤ You can also fold ⑤ from **Windmill** (p. 40).

⑥ **Coaster I**

Begin with **Windmill** (p. 40).

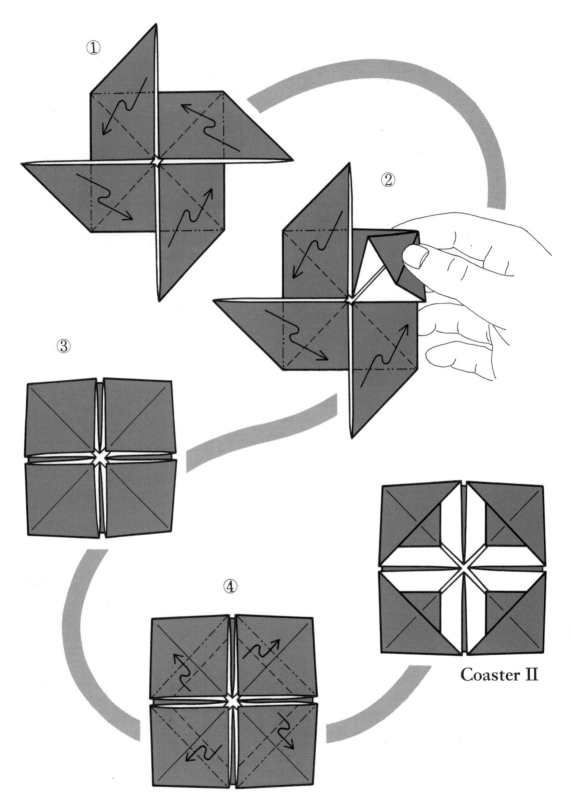

① ② ③ ④

Coaster II

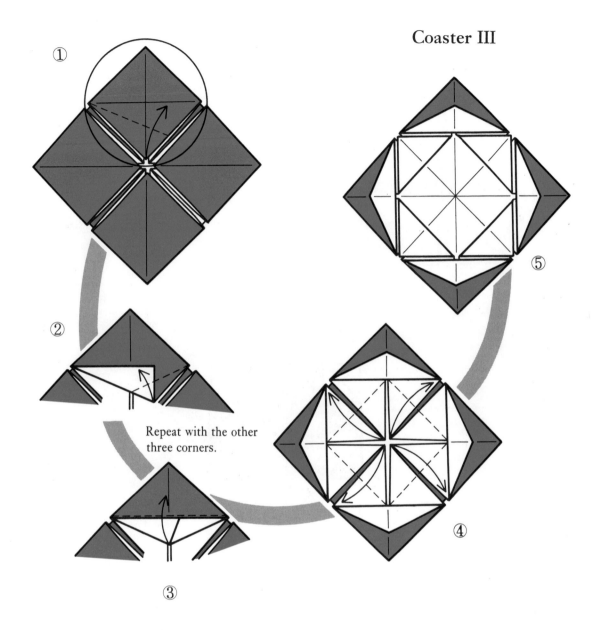

Coaster III

① ② ③

Repeat with the other three corners.

④ ⑤

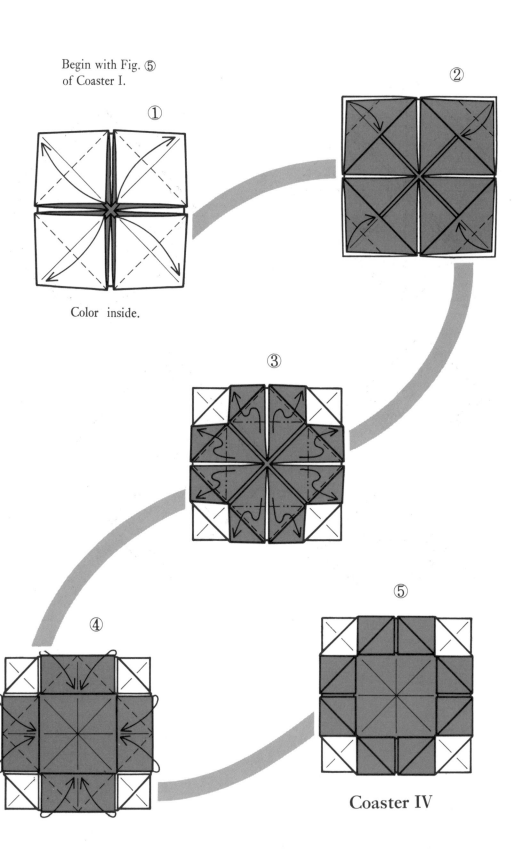

Begin with Fig. ⑤
of Coaster I.

① Color inside.

②

③

④

⑤

Coaster IV

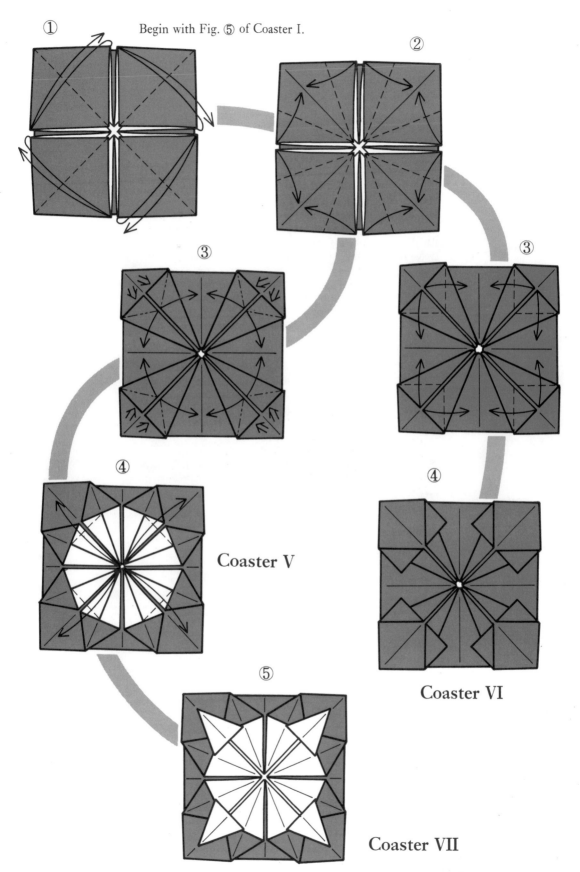

① Begin with Fig. ⑤ of Coaster I.

②

③

③

④

Coaster V

④

Coaster VI

⑤

Coaster VII

Author :   TOSHIE TAKAHAMA

1908:   Born in Tokyo.
1930:   Graduated from Tsuda College.
1946–1965:   Worked for the Foreign News Section of the Japan
                 Broadcasting Corporation (NHK) as a newswriter.
1965:   Retired from NHK.
1966–1971:   Worked for the Asia Foundation, Tokyo.
1965:   Visited the U.S.A. to demonstrate origami at the
                 Japan Pavilion for the World Fair in New York,
                 developing friendships with American folders at
                 various places.
1968:   Held the first exhibition of foreign folders' works
                 in Tokyo.

                 Visited Europe and the British Origami Society in
                 London (1974), China (1979), Formosa (1980), and
                 Italy and France (1981) on goodwill missions.
1976:   Joined the 1st Origami World Fair held by the
                 Nippon Origami Ass'n; working for every event on
                 this level since that time.
1978:   Joined the World Fair in Mexico.
1982:   Visited Singapore joining the origami tour sponsored
                 by NOA.

1984:   Visited San Francisco and Los Angeles, and
                 held six origami classes.

Membership: Director of NOA (RIJI)
                 Member of the Origami Center of America (New York)
                 Member of the British Origami Society
                 President of the Origami Study Group (Tokyo)

Works: "Creative Life with Creative Origami I"
                 "Creative Life with Creative Origami II"
                 "Origami for Fun"
                 "Origami Toys"
                 "Origami for Displays"
                 And 15 others.

Address: 24–1, Matsunoki 3-chome, Suginami-ku, Tokyo, 166
Telephone: (03) 311–8130

Origami Symbols & Procedures

Outline and Crease

Concealed part or
previous position

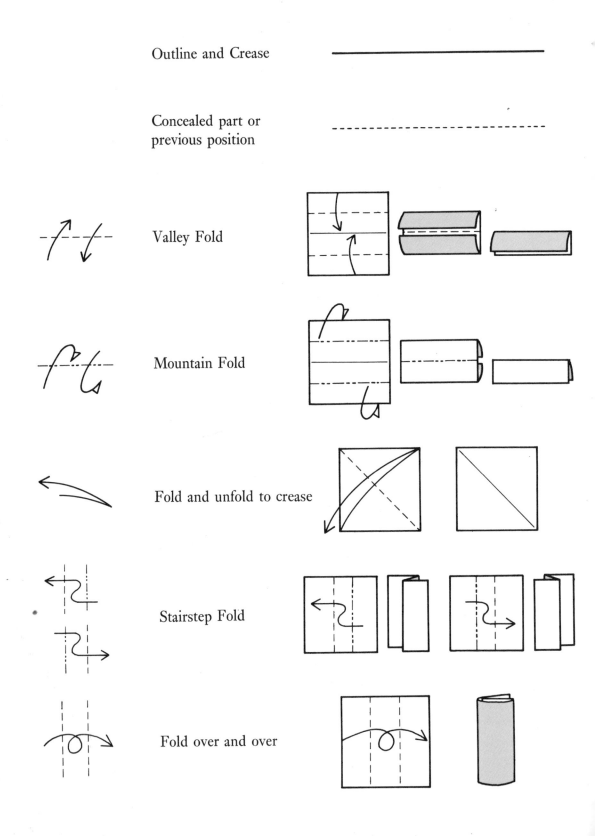

Valley Fold

Mountain Fold

Fold and unfold to crease

Stairstep Fold

Fold over and over

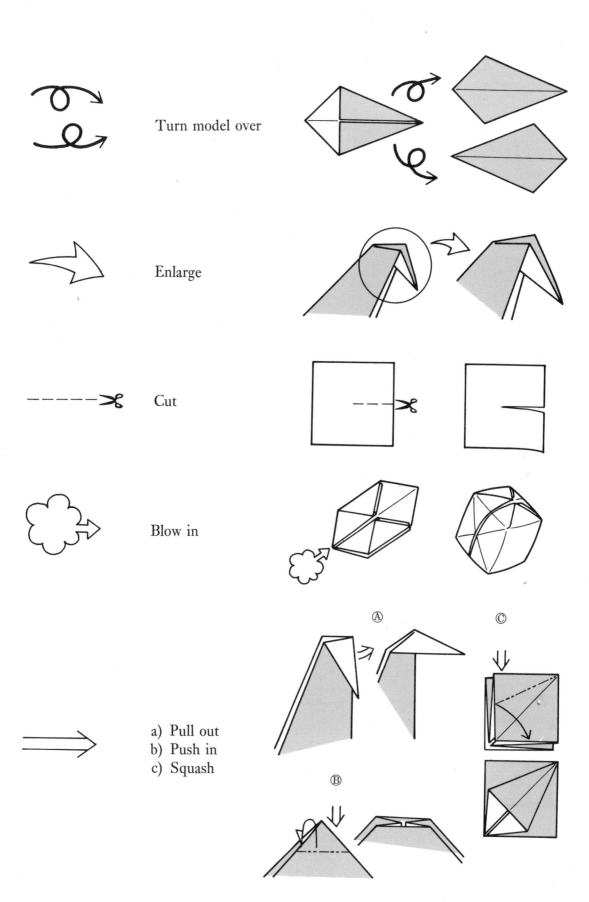

Turn model over

Enlarge

Cut

Blow in

a) Pull out
b) Push in
c) Squash